PUBLICATION NUMBER 14
Duke University Commonwealth-Studies Center

The Growth of Canadian Policies
in External Affairs

Duke University Commonwealth-Studies Center Publications

1. *The British Commonwealth: An Experiment in Co-operation among Nations,* by Frank H. Underhill
2. *South Africa: Economic and Political Aspects,* by Hector Menteith Robertson
3. *Some Comparative Aspects of Irish Law,* by Alfred Gaston Donaldson
4. *Economic Analysis and Policy in Underdeveloped Countries,* by P. T. Bauer
5. *The Higher Public Service of the Commonwealth of Australia,* by Howard A. Scarrow
6. *Economic Opinion and Policy in Ceylon,* by Henry M. Oliver, Jr.
7. *Problems of the New Commonwealth,* by Sir Ivor Jennings
8. *Commonwealth Perspectives,* by Nicholas Mansergh *et al.*
9. *Evolving Canadian Federalism,* by A. R. M. Lower, F. R. Scott, *et al.*
10. *The Commonwealth Economy in Southeast Asia,* by T. H. Silcock
11. *Public Expenditures in Australia,* by B. U. Ratchford
12. *The American Economic Impact on Canada,* by Hugh G. J. Aitken, John J. Deutsch, W. A. Mackintosh, *et al.*
13. *Tradition, Values, and Socio-Economic Development,* edited by Ralph Braibanti and J. J. Spengler
14. *The Growth of Canadian Policies in External Affairs,* by Hugh L. Keenleyside *et al.*

The Growth of Canadian Policies
in External Affairs

Hugh L. Keenleyside, James Eayrs,
Gaddis Smith, David R. Deener,
Gérard Bergeron, Vincent W. Bladen,
Edgar McInnis

Duke University, Durham, N.C.
Commonwealth-Studies Center.

PUBLISHED FOR THE

Duke University Commonwealth-Studies Center

DUKE UNIVERSITY PRESS, DURHAM, N. C.

CAMBRIDGE UNIVERSITY PRESS, LONDON

1960

© 1960, Duke University Press

Library of Congress Catalogue Card Number
60-13605

Cambridge University Press, London N.W. 1, England

PRINTED IN THE UNITED STATES OF AMERICA

BY THE SEEMAN PRINTERY, INC., DURHAM, N. C.

CONTRIBUTORS

DR. HUGH L. KEENLEYSIDE—Chairman of the British Columbia Power Commission; recently Under-Secretary for Public Administration in the United Nations following extended service as Director-General of the Technical Assistance Administration of the United Nations; wide experience in Canadian external affairs and service abroad.

JAMES G. EAYRS—Assistant Professor of Political Economy, University of Toronto; Editor, *Canadian Journal of Economics and Political Science* and Co-editor, *The International Journal* (Canadian Quarterly).

GADDIS SMITH—Instructor in History, Duke University, Durham, North Carolina.

DAVID R. DEENER—Professor of Political Science, Tulane University, New Orleans, Louisiana; author of *The United States Attorneys General and International Law.*

GÉRARD BERGERON—Professeur Agrégés, Faculté des Sciences sociales, L'Université Laval (Quebec); analyst and commentator on political affairs for television and the press.

VINCENT W. BLADEN—Professor of Political Economy and Dean of the Faculty of Arts, University of Toronto; Past-President of The Canadian Political Science Association and for many years Managing Editor of *The Canadian Journal of Economics and Political Science.*

EDGAR MCINNIS—educator, historian, author; President, Canadian Institute of International Affairs; long-time member of the Department of History, University of Toronto; member of the Canadian delegation to the United Nations (1952); most recent book, *The Atlantic Triangle and the Cold War* (1959).

FOREWORD

THE APPEARANCE in the era of two World Wars of the Commonwealth of Nations as the heir to what was once the British Empire has not been given in the United States the attention it merits as a field for study. It was in response to this need that a Commonwealth-Studies Center was created at Duke University in 1955 with financial assistance from the Carnegie Corporation. The Center is devoted to the encouragement of research in Commonwealth affairs by members of the Duke University faculty and graduate students, and to the encouragement of similar research in economics, history, and political science by scholars and graduate students from various Commonwealth countries.

The purposes of the Center are implemented in a number of ways. Among these is the annual program known as the Commonwealth Summer Seminar and Research Group, which in each of the summers of 1956, 1957, 1958, and 1959 brought to the University for a period of two months groups of scholars already known for their interest and competence in one or another aspect of Commonwealth affairs. During the summer these scholars in residence pursued their own research in their chosen fields. They came together daily around the coffee table for informal discussion of their research projects or of more general Commonwealth topics. In addition, the group met formally at intervals as a seminar for critical analysis of papers prepared by distinguished visiting Canadian and American lecturers.

In the summer of 1959 the visiting lecturers presented papers on the growth of Canadian policies and procedures in external affairs. In these more formal sessions, as well as in the daily informal meetings, the visiting scholars were joined by interested members of the Duke University faculty.

The Summer Seminar and Research Group program has thus sought to further a number of useful purposes. It has provided a means whereby a limited number of scholars who are university teachers with Commonwealth interests may pursue their research throughout a summer unimpeded by the demands of classroom instruction. It has given them an opportunity for informal association with others of similar interests for

the free exchange and stimulation of ideas.   Finally, in centering attention on a particular theme during a given summer, it has brought to the
Seminar, and to the wider audience to which these pages are addressed,
some of the mature thought of scholars whose understanding of political, economic, constitutional, and social forces, as these have been operating between Canada and the outside world, is penetrating as well as
comprehensive.

The essays here presented have been edited for publication by Professor
John S. Gillespie, Executive Secretary of the Commonwealth-Studies Center, 1958-1959.

Since the Commonwealth-Studies Center is concerned exclusively with
the encouragement of research, any interpretations of Commonwealth
developments appearing in its publications do not represent expressions of
the views of the Center or of the Carnegie Corporation; the authors of
the several publications are responsible for the conclusions expressed in
them.

PAUL H. CLYDE, *Chairman*
The Summer Seminar and
Research Group

CONTENTS

CONTENTS

*The Growth of Canadian Policies
in External Affairs*

Introduction

Hugh L. Keenleyside

IT IS DIFFICULT to generalize accurately about any country, though as a witty Frenchman once said, "All generalizations are untrue, including this one." In contemporary life in the United States for example, illustrations can be found to contradict almost any statement no matter how moderate or how extreme, whether of good or bad. But it is even more difficult to generalize justly about Canada. Its population is more varied than that of the United States; its proportion of new arrivals is larger. Its religious divisions are more extensive—although, on the whole, they seem to cause less concern.

Canadians as a people—to generalize—are less single minded than their southern neighbors. They do not so readily see everything in black or white—or red. Their own historical figures are not sharply divided, as are the Americans', between the Good Guys and the Bad. They have no George Washington or Abraham Lincoln; no Benedict Arnold or Aaron Burr. Neither do Canadians view the contemporary world in these simple terms of absolute contrast. With regard to the United States, for instance, they admire that country and usually like the individual American, but tend to look askance at some aspects of the public policies of the Republic. Recently they have sometimes been almost terrified by the way in which those policies have been expressed by some of the more bellicose American admirals, generals, and politicians, and by the brink-balancing of the late Mr. Secretary Dulles. (In this fondness for the individual combined with dislike for official policy Canadians are not, perhaps, so very different from the Americans themselves, who almost unanimously like Ike, but vote robustly against his party and his policies.)

One of the more obvious differences between Canadians—to continue to generalize—and Americans is that the former take much more interest in international affairs than is customary in the United States. This is due in part to the fact that Canadian life is more directly and gravely affected by what goes on elsewhere than has been the case with the enormously powerful and considerably more nearly self-sufficient Republic. Canadian prosperity depends far more on foreign trade and on what goes on in foreign countries (especially in the United States) than does American. The New Yorker, the San Franciscan, the Bostonian do not need to be particularly worried by what the Canadian Parliament may be doing in Ottawa, even though Canada is by long odds the best customer of the United States. But the Vancouverite, the Montrealer, or the Haligonian are frequently and very intimately affected by policies being debated in Washington.

Again, as part of a world-wide political association—the Commonwealth—Canadians are likely to be concerned rather more than are their neighbors about such places as India and Pakistan, South Africa and New Zealand. Because of their continuing political, constitutional, and still sentimental attachment to the "Old Country," Canadians study more British history and have more British news in their papers and magazines and over the air than do most Americans. Canadian newspapers even publish regularly the results of British football (soccer) games! As a result it is a rather firmly established tradition in academic, journalistic, and even social circles in Canada that foreign affairs are among the subjects in which an interest can acceptably be displayed. In the more sophisticated circles it is almost smart to be intelligently informed.

A final reason for the comparatively widespread interest of Canadians in foreign affairs is the fact that their management of their own part in these high matters is a very recent development. The construction and execution of a foreign policy is a new and rather intriguing experience. The Honorable Lester B. Pearson, for example, although still far from decrepitude, was one of those who took the first examination for admission to the Canadian foreign service. The Right Honorable Vincent Massey, who only recently retired as Governor-General, was the first Canadian diplomat to serve abroad. It is not surprising that it is fashionable for Canadians to be interested in this new national adventure.

The usual American reaction to issues of foreign policy, on the contrary, is one of comparative indifference—except when passions are aroused by some specific and temporary crisis. Perhaps President Eisenhower exaggerated a little when he said in September, 1959, that when dealing with the problems of international life, "You have to tackle [the American people] and hold them down to feed these facts to them." But it is a complaint frequently heard in Washington.

Yet, paradoxically, Canadians do not become as emotionally aroused about international problems as do Americans—on the infrequent occasions when the latter do think about such subjects. This is probably due in part to the fact, mentioned above, that Canadians do not find it easy to think of all foreigners—or all Canadians either—as entirely good or entirely bad. Even the Russians are looked upon as being somewhat less than universally malevolent. Since before World War I there has probably been, among Canadians, a more widespread dislike of Germany than of any other foreign country. But even this has been so diluted by perplexity over how the civilized Germans could erupt into the Hitlerite abominations that the Canadian feeling cannot be described as a complete and undiluted antipathy.

An obvious reason for the comparative restraint of Canadians in foreign affairs is that they recognize, unhappily and sometimes a little resentfully, that there is not very much that Ottawa can do to influence the course of events. Since 1939 Canada has in fact carried a good deal more weight in the international community than might have been expected from a country of less than twenty million people. Proportionately to size there is no other country, with the possible exception of Sweden, that has exercised anything like a comparable influence. This has been due in part to the exceptional abilities of Mr. Pearson. But if Mr. Pearson had not existed it would probably have been necessary to invent him, because Canadians, aroused by the insanity of World War II, had things to say and, in the early post-war years, Canada had just enough prestige to insure an interested audience. As a result of Mr. Pearson's remarkable talents that prestige enormously increased.

But since the division of the world between two centers of overwhelming power, Canada, on all fundamental issues, has had to fall in with American policy. It is probable that a great majority of Canadians would like to get away from their present tight political and defense ties with the United States. Many Canadians would like their country to become a North American Switzerland or Sweden. Within recent months the most widely read newspaper in Canada and the national magazine with the largest circulation have both shown an active and sympathetic interest in proposals for Canadian withdrawal from any participation in preparations for nuclear warfare and from the existing satellite relationship to Washington in defence matters. Every month sees new journalistic recruits enrolled in support of such a change. However, an independent Canadian line in such matters is still considered impractical, if not intrinsically dangerous and wrong, by most of those in national posts of political responsibility. Whether this opposition will be or can be maintained will depend on how soon American policy begins to show results in the relaxation of present tensions and the diminution of present dangers. Any long continuance of what most Canadians consider to be the present intransigent American policy of demanding everything and conceding nothing will result in a rapid increase in demands for Canadian withdrawal from the existing relationship.

It is Canada's fortune—good or bad—to have come on the international stage at a time when anything like complete autonomy in foreign policies is a rapidly vanishing concept and an even more rapidly disappearing reality. Within the limits thus prescribed, however, Canadians do strive to design and express a foreign policy of their own.

Given these facts it is most seemly that the Duke University Commonwealth-Studies Center should be responsible for a volume on the Development of Canadian Policies in External Affairs. This is particularly true because in many ways Canada has blazed the trail being followed by other Commonwealth countries in their progress along this path.

* * *

Prior to World War I Canada had done little to express any native views on foreign policy. It is true that Canadians had sworn, more or less under their breath, at the way in which they believed— for the most part quite wrongly—that Britain had sacrificed Canadian interests on the altar of Anglo-American friendship. But the background of Canadian thinking in the nineteenth century even on such a fundamental problem as relations with the United States was wholly inadequate, and much of the thinking itself almost incredibly naïve. For example the generally astute Prime Minister Sir John A. Macdonald wrote in 1867:

War will come some day between England and the United States and India can do us yeoman's service by sending an army of Sikhs, Ghoorkas and Belochees etc., etc., across the Pacific to San Francisco and holding that beautiful and immoral city with the surrounding California as security for Montreal and Canada.

It is, of course, understandable that the events of the sixties should have caused deep fear of the United States in Canada, but Sir John's prescription for meeting the danger betrayed a vast ignorance of international realities.

Even when Sir Wilfrid Laurier came to power in 1896 he was unable, or believed that he was unable, successfully to challenge the jingoistic popular demand in the English-speaking provinces that Canada should assist Britain in the disgraceful war against the Boers. The colonial sentiment that provoked this decision was to bear bitter fruit in venomous discord between many extremists among English and French Canadians during the First World War.

The ultimate effect of Canadian participation in 1914-1918, however, was a tremendous impetus to the growth of Canadian nationalism. The way for such a development had been prepared by the vast immigration movement of the years between the opening of the century and 1914. This tide from Europe filled in many of the gaps in the central Provinces and swept on into western Canada, where it was joined by another stream of immigrants coming in from the central and western states where the "frontier" had substantially disappeared by 1890. Most of these immigrants knew and cared little about Britain and the Empire; they wanted farms, freedom, new homes in a new land. The prosperity of these years as contrasted with the almost continuous depression of the early decades after Confederation strengthened the spirit of nationalism in Canada— a spirit that was encouraged by the growing self-sufficiency of Canadian life and the pride that accompanied the conquest of half a continent. This was illustrated in contrasting ways by the fact that Canadians felt disposed to rebuff the United States over the reciprocity proposal in 1911 and by the extreme difficulty experienced in 1912 and 1913 by the new Conservative Government in getting parliamentary—or indeed popular—approval for the administration's plan to contribute major units to the British Navy.

But when war broke out in 1914 Canadians, except in Quebec, went in willingly and even, in many instances, with the enthusiasm of patriotic ignorance. But the inevitable effect of the conflict

——of the pride in their country and confidence in themselves which were evoked by the outstanding record of the Canadian volunteers;

——of the repeated disregard of Canadian views and interests by the military and political authorities in London;

——of the economic strain imposed by the conflict; and, above all,

——of the deadly, dragging, acrid misery of the war itself

all caused a revolution in feeling in Canada that found deep expression in the demands for a more complete exercise of self-government after the war.

In no one was this change more marked than in the case of the Prime Minister himself. Sir Robert Borden, who in 1914 was still largely colonial in spirit and policy, came out of the war as one of the great architects of Canadian nationhood—a transformation that has been too little recognized by Canadian historians. (It would, perhaps, have been more clearly understood if the official life of this great Canadian had not omitted some of Sir Robert's strongest expressions of his new point of view.) It is true that even at the end of the war Borden's concept of the Commonwealth still permitted a "single voice" in foreign affairs; but it also required a fair consideration of Canadian and other Dominion views as to what that voice should say. It remained for Mr. Mackenzie King and General Hertzog of South Africa to win acceptance of the principle that Commonwealth countries could speak with many and, if they so desired, with conflicting tongues.

During the postwar years the road of Canadian autonomy rose quickly from the valley of colonialism. The separate, though still subordinate, signature of the Peace Treaty—against the vigorous protests, not now of London, but of the President of the United States; Canadian insistence on the abrogation of the Anglo-Japanese Alliance; the refusal to support Lloyd George in his threatened war against the Turks in 1922; the independent signature of the Halibut Treaty with the U.S.A. in 1923; the refusal to be bound by the Locarno agreements; the establishment of a Canadian diplomatic service in 1927-1928; the Balfour Declaration of 1926 and its implication in the Statute of Westminster in 1931; the change in the Coronation Oath in 1936; the independent and delayed declaration of war against Germany in 1939; and the independent and first declaration of war against Japan in 1941 were all mileposts of progress in Canadian nationalism.

. . .

Unfortunately this growth of national independence was not matched by the development of an enlightened, idealistic, and realistic (in this case they would have marched together) policy in the realm of foreign affairs. Indeed during the interwar years Canadian policy towards the League of Nations and towards European and Asian problems generally could hardly have been less helpful, or more misguided.

With regard to the political problems of Europe Canadians in effect confined themselves for twenty years to composing and declaiming censorious lectures about the depravity of the governments and the peoples of the Old World in contrast, sometimes by implication but often in plain or florid terms, with the virtues of the New. Britain, of course, was generally excepted.

It is perhaps true that internal stresses within Canada made a more enlightened and more positive policy in foreign affairs impossible. But it is at least arguable that if the government had made any serious effort to give leadership in the interpretation of the international scene the Canadian people, French-speaking and English-speaking alike, might have responded with the humanity and intelligence which marked many other aspects of Canadian life. But the governments of the day, especially under Prime Minister Mackenzie King, consistently blocked all attempts to establish a tradition of informed debate on international affairs in the Canadian Parliament. The Prime Minister almost invariably delayed the introduction of the External Affairs estimates until the tired and impatient days at the end of the Parliamentary session. He would then make one long, prolix speech saying in effect that Canada had no responsibility for the sad state of affairs in the world, that in any case these conditions were no threat to Canadian security, and that the best thing that Parliament could do would be to say little and to take no sides. This annual scene was described by one acute Canadian observer, Edgar J. Tarr, in the following terms:

There comes to mind the juggler who, with great dexterity, keeps several balls in the air. The balls are Isolationism, North Americanism, Imperialism and Collectivism. One sees them going up and coming down with rhythmic regularity, and suddenly they are lost in polished phrases of a platitudinous peroration—the magician's handkerchief."

As to policy the Prime Minister would commit himself to nothing except that in case of a crisis arising "Parliament would decide."

It was not until World War II was imminent that Mr. King took a clearer stand on the European crisis that was spreading its minatory shadows on all the world. When he did commit himself he could hardly have been more wrong. He praised extravagantly the policy of appeasement and at the same time gave broad reason for Hitler to doubt that Canada would, in any circumstances, intervene in a European conflict. He supported a foreign policy that made war inevitable but at home he refused to take any serious steps to prepare for Canadian participation. That this was at the same time the policy of successive British and French governments was little excuse for Canada. At least some small measure of objectivity might reasonably have been expected from Ottawa. But the administration, without any significant complaint from the official opposition, had so dulled and so misled Canadian opinion that only one important paper in the whole Dominion—the *Free Press* of Winnipeg—opposed the stupid dishonesty of Munich.

To what extent Mr. King's misreading of the European situation was the result of the influence of Canadian representatives, to what degree it was affected by the Prime Minister's extensive personal correspondence with Canadian expatriates and other acquaintances among the most conservative elements in the social circles of London, and in what measure it was the result of his own temperament, can only be a matter of opinion. It is probable that all were at work.

Not content with misreading the European prospect, Mr. King, and Prime Minister Bennett during the Tory interregnum from 1930 to 1935, were equally misguided in their estimate of the course of events in the Far East. They would have nothing to do with any proposal for intervention by the League of Nations in an attempt to contain Japan when the military leaders of that country raised the curtain on a decade of aggression by the carefully stage-managed incident at Mukden in September, 1931. When Sir John Simon, the most coldly ardent apologist for Japan, defended Tokyo in Geneva he was seconded by no one so warmly as by the Canadian Conservative, C. H. Cahan. Later, and up until a few days before Pearl Harbor, Mr. King was accepting the opinion of the British Ambassador—a singularly inept incumbent—and of Mr. Joseph Grew that a few little concessions to Japan would relieve the tension in that quarter and that no harm would be done. After all, the apologists argued, somebody had to bring order in China! So aggression prospered not only without official Canadian opposition but in spite of widespread popular protest, and with the aid of unrestricted supplies of Canadian scrap iron and nickel!

During these two decades the League of Nations was viewed by the Canadian government—not, obviously, without some justification—as a European instrument, controlled by Europeans, and used (when used at all) for European ends. On this basis Canada, while retaining membership, did everything possible to eliminate the only provisions in the Covenant, and in the gradually developing traditions of the League, that gave hope of its becoming something more. Canadian representatives tried to remove and, failing that, to interpret away, Article X. When faced with the possibility that the League might actually begin to function in accordance with its announced principles and duties (in the Far East and Ethiopia for example) Canada was urgent in opposition.

It can be conceded that Mr. King was right in arguing that Canada had little responsibility for the conditions that made these aggressions possible and even inevitable for, of course, this was true. At worst Canada, without having created the dangers and being unable by herself to change the world, merely acquiesced in the policies followed in relation to Japan, Ethiopia, Spain, and Germany, and towards the purposes and uses of the League itself, by the Governments of Britain, France, Italy, and the United States; policies expounded most ably if also most callously by "the worst foreign minister in British history." If the countries most directly concerned and because of their power most responsible were unwilling to act, why should Canada take a stand?

But before accepting these excuses it is worth recalling that New Zealand, faced with the same problems, was consistent and persistent in trying to convince the Europeans and other signers of the Covenant that the members of the League should take their pledged words seriously. If politics is the art of the immediately possible this was probably bad politics. But at least it set an example of honesty in a singularly dishonest period of international relations. The New Zealand government did what one government could do to raise the standard of morality in an era that was setting new records for political degradation. It would have been gratifying to have been able to say as much of Canada. This is particularly true in light of the ultimate utter failure of the policy of expedient dishonesty.

The proof that Canada should have been concerned is found in the fact that the failure of the League brought many thousands of Canadians to their death in another war. It is true that Canadian efforts would almost certainly have failed, as did those of the sister Dominion. But New Zealand at least tried.

. . .

If World War I gave the final impetus towards the achievement of Canadian national autonomy, World War II impelled the Canadian government to take a more realistic attitude towards, and a more active participation in, the whole gamut of international affairs. It can plausibly be argued that Mr. King's greatest contribution to Canadian history was his emphasis on the development of, and on the maintenance of high standards in, the new service that made this participation possible.

In 1925 Canada had a High Commissioner in London and a similar functionary in Paris. Neither was accorded diplomatic recognition and neither was given any very significant functions to perform. In Ottawa the senior staff of the Department of External Affairs could be counted on the fingers of one hand—with a couple of fingers left over. It was not until 1927 that the first Canadian diplomatic post was established abroad (in Washington), and it was not until the following year that regular recruitment for the foreign service was initiated.

By 1939 Canada had sixteen diplomatic and consular posts abroad; in 1959 there are sixty-two. In the 1920's and 1930's Canada sought to reduce still further the almost negligible influence of the League of Nations; since 1945 Canada has been one of the most active proponents of a strong and effective United Nations, and NATO might almost be said to be a Canadian invention. In 1920 Canada was an insignificant member of the world community to whom no one needed, and few bothered, to pay attention; in recent years it is probably not an exaggeration to say that with the exception of the two world-dominating powers, and perhaps (but only perhaps) the United Kingdom and India, Canada can be, and on occasion has been, the most influential member of the world organization.

. . .

Within the special community of the Commonwealth Canada has recently played an active and exceptionally significant role. This was never so well exemplified as in 1956, when a seriously ill Prime Minister plunged the United Kingdom into an adventure in the Middle East which, utterly senseless as an instrument for the achievement of any of its announced and contradictory purposes, and horrifying as it was to all rational opinion at home and abroad, had the added danger of being a threat to the continued existence of the Commonwealth itself. Canadian action in that crisis provided leadership in finding a solution that was acceptable to world opinion and at the same time convinced the colored nations of the Commonwealth that that association was not a club of which they were only second-class members. If it is too much to say that Canada saved the Commonwealth it is obviously true that Canadian action maintained it in a strength and spirit that had been in imminent danger of being destroyed.

Canada's influence for good in the Commonwealth has been further strengthened by the prominent role of Canadian dollars and Canadian personnel in the Colombo Plan activities and by the warmth with which Canada under both Liberal and Conservative administrations has welcomed new members from Asia and Africa into full membership in the association.

. . .

It is well that these matters should be examined, and it is both gratifying and indicative that such an examination should be undertaken under American academic auspices with Canadian participation. The future of the Commonwealth and Canada's role as an independent nation participating fully in both the Commonwealth and in the wider association of the United Nations are of real significance not only to the United States but to all nations of the still free world. Only good can come from a clearer knowledge of such matters and any increase in understanding is a cause for rejoicing in these tense and troubled times.

The Origins of Canada's Department of External Affairs*

James Eayrs

I.

Although on June 1, 1959, Canada's Department of External Affairs could look back upon a history of half a century's duration,[1] it is not the oldest of such departments in the overseas Commonwealth, a distinction belonging to the Australian Department of External Affairs created with the new federation in 1901.[2] The Australian innovation excited no interest in Canada, despite the appearance during the same year of a book by a Canadian author containing what is probably the earliest written advocacy of separate foreign ministries for the self-governing colonies or dominions.[3] Soon after the publication of this work, if not before, the idea of creating some form of Canadian foreign office had occurred to Joseph

* This paper is a revised version of "The Origins of Canada's Department of External Affairs," *Canadian Journal of Economics and Political Science*, XXV (May 1959), 109-128. I am grateful to the University of Toronto Press for permission to make use here of material originally appearing in that article.

[1] The Act creating a Department of External Affairs was brought into force by a proclamation issued on the evening of June 1, 1909, by authority of Order-in-Council P.C. 1227 of June 1, 1909.

[2] "The useful and varied activities of this pioneer Australian department, however, only rarely touched on the field of diplomacy. The Australian department can claim priority of name but it was to be the Canadian department which gave 'External Affairs' the connotation it now possesses throughout the Commonwealth." K. A. MacKirdy, "The First Australian Department of External Affairs: 1901-16," *Canadian Journal of Economics and Political Science*, XXV (Nov. 1959), 507.

[3] W. Sanford Evans, *The Canadian Contingents and Canadian Imperialism* (London, 1901). Evans, a Manitoba Conservative, a journalist and financier, was mayor of Winnipeg in 1909-1910. His early advocacy of separate foreign offices for the overseas Dominions has been pointed out in F. H. Soward, *The Department of External Affairs and Canadian Autonomy, 1899-1939*, Canadian Historical Association Booklet No. 7 (Ottawa, 1956), p. 5.

Pope, one of the nation's most experienced public servants, who as Under Secretary of State since 1896 had attended to a wide range of governmental business, much of it relating to external affairs.[4] He took a keen and solitary interest in the fate of official documents, striving to rescue them from oblivion and to arrange them in some sort of order for future reference; and it was this aspect of negotiation which first aroused his concern for establishing what he later referred to as "a more systematic mode of dealing with what I may term, for want of a better phrase, the *external affairs* of the Dominion."[5] It was while working on the Canadian case for the Alaska Boundary dispute that Pope became aware of the inadequacy of the Dominion's facilities. "I have been looking into the subject," he wrote to John Anderson of the Colonial Office in 1899, "but it is a case of making bricks without straw. I find the greatest difficulty in collecting the papers necessary to a proper understanding of the case. Are there any blue books published about 1888 at home containing the correspondence of that period? . . . I dare say you may be surprised at my requests for what are elementary papers, but . . . we sadly lack system here."[6] Eight years later there had been little improvement. "We are much handicapped here," the Governor-General, Earl Grey, wrote to the British Ambassador at Washington, "by the want of any organized Department for the coordination and reproduction of information bearing on the relations between Canada and the U.S. It happens that Mr. Pope the Under Secretary of State has taken a personal interest in this question and has got together from time to time a certain, but by no means complete, collection of papers."[7]

The first formal advocacy of what was to become the Department of External Affairs is contained in a lengthy memorandum submitted

[4] Joseph Pope had been private secretary to Sir John A. Macdonald from 1882 to 1891; assistant clerk of the Privy Council; and, since 1896, Under Secretary of State. In 1893 he served on the staff of the British Agent at the Behring Sea Arbitration in Paris; in 1898-1899 he took part in the work of the Joint High Commission in Quebec and Washington; and in 1903 he was an associate secretary at the Alaska Boundary Tribunal in London. See Maurice Pope (ed.), *Public Servant: The Memoirs of Sir Joseph Pope* (Toronto, 1960).

[5] "Memorandum for Consideration of the Civil Service Commissioners, 25 May, 1907," Civil Service Commission 1908: Minutes of Evidence, I, p. 48, *Sessional Papers of Canada*, XLII, no. 15, 1907-1908.

[6] July 10, 1899, Pope Papers (Public Archives of Canada), "Alaska Boundary Correspondence," I, 18.

[7] Grey to James Bryce, Jan. 14, 1907, Grey Papers (P.A.C.), box 14, folder 12a.

by Pope to the Royal Commission on the Civil Service on May 25, 1907. "The preparation of despatches," he noted,

is a technical acquirement, attained only after special study of the questions involved, and by assiduous practice in drafting. It may happen; it must sometimes happen; that the official to whom these Imperial despatches are referred (for it cannot be expected that a busy Minister has time to attend to such matters personally, calling for much study, and a large acquaintance with intricate details) while fully competent to deal with the merits of the question in its present aspect, is not familiar with the past history of the controversy or skilled in the framing of State papers. There are moreover certain questions which relate partly to one department and partly to another, so that it may not be easy to tell at first sight to whom a new despatch should be referred. . . .

In the early years of Confederation, when these questions were few, the inconvenience of which I speak was not so greatly felt, as the Prime Minister of the day kept them pretty much in his own hands; but with the growth and development of the Dominion this is no longer possible.

The practical result of the system in vogue is that there does not exist to-day in any department a complete record of the correspondence to which I have alluded. It has been so scattered, and passed through so many hands that there is no approach to continuity in any of the departmental files. Such knowledge concerning them as is available, is, for the most part, lodged in the memories of a few officials. I fear too that in Downing Street, Canadian despatches are noted for diversity rather than for elegance of style. As the Dominion grows this state of things must always be getting worse. If some reform is not soon effected it will be too late. Even now, I am of opinion that it would be an extremely difficult task to construct from our official files anything approaching to a complete record of any of the international questions in which Canada has been concerned during the past fifty years. . . .

My suggestion is, that all despatches relating to external affairs should be referred by the Privy Council to one department, whose staff should contain men trained in the study of these questions, and in the conduct of diplomatic correspondence. These officials should be in close touch with the other department, from which they could draw all necessary information, the raw material, as it were, of their work; but the digesting of this information, and its presentation in diplomatic form, should rest with them, through, of course, the same channels as at present; for in this suggestion there is no thought of change in that regard. Every effort should be made to collect from the beginning all papers bearing on the questions I have indicated, from the office of the Governor General, the Privy Council office, the various departments and the Foreign and Colonial offices. I wish most earnestly to impress upon all concerned that if this work is not soon systematically begun it will be too late. The few men throughout the service conversant with these questions are growing old, and must soon disappear. So far as I know they will leave no successors. Much of the early history of these subjects, so far as Canadian records are concerned, will thus be lost.

I recommend that a small staff of young men, well educated and carefully selected, be attached to the department whose creation I have advocated, and that they be specially trained in the knowledge and treatment of these subjects. In this way we shall acquire an organized method of dealing with international questions which at present we wholly lack.

I have spoken of the creation of another department, but I see no reason why this work should not be done under the supervision of the Secretary of State, whose present department might be divided into two sections, one for Canadian, and one for External affairs. . . .[8]

Copies of the Pope memorandum were sent to various members of the government. There is record of only one response, this from L. P. Brodeur, the Minister of Marine and Naval Defence, who wrote to say that he was "very favourably impressed with your arguments, and they are exactly in accord with my own views."[9] An opportunity to influence another member of the Cabinet came later in the year when Pope accompanied Rodolphe Lemieux, who was both Minister of Labour and Postmaster General in the Laurier Government, on his mission to Japan with the object of negotiating a "Gentleman's Agreement" regarding the number of immigrants which the Japanese government would allow to proceed to Canada. During such appropriate intervals as may have presented themselves in the course of their "long stormy passage across the Pacific, the worst our Captain had known on that route,"[10] Pope informed Lemieux of his difficulties in the past and of his hopes for the future. Lemieux was not unreceptive, and his experience while conducting negotiations in Tokyo only strengthened the force of Pope's argu-

[8] Reproduced in full in Eayrs, *op. cit.*, pp. 111-113.
[9] Brodeur to Pope, Oct. 21, 1907, Under Secretary of State: Semi-Official Correspondence (P.A.C.), folder 191.
[10] Pope to Sir Wilfrid Laurier, Nov. 15, 1907, Laurier Papers (P.A.C.), 132091-2.

ments. "En lisant la correspondance échangée entre Tokio, Londres et Ottawa depuis 1894," Lemieux wrote from Japan,

il est malheureusement trop évident que nous n'avons suivi, au Canada, les négociations d'assez près. Nous pouvions—au début—obtenir des *Concessions* et c'est à peine si nous avons répondue par un accusé de réception aux propositions avantageuses qui nous étaient faites! Nous manquons absolument de tradition et de correction. L'affaire de tout le monde n'est l'affaire de personne. J'en ai long à vous dire la-dessus. Je n'ai pu obtenir à Ottawa que des bribes de documents et de correspondances, ce rapportant à ce traité. Il faut voir au contraire commes les *records* du F.O. à Londres sont parfaits et comme la genèse du traité en est complète. J'ai ou mettre la main sur ces records (12 *vols.* semblables aux factums de la Cour d'Appel). *"Forewarned is forearmed"*. C'est un consultant tout cela que j'ai cause, tout en évitant d'aborder ceux qui nous étaient défavorables. Il faudra que Sir W. [Laurier] réorganise dans le service public tout ce qui a trait à la correspondance officielle. Il ne faut plus qu'elle soit repartie entre les différents ministères. Tout devrait être remis au Secrétaire d'Etat et nous aurions alors des *Records* intelligibles.

Tout ceci pour dire que si, comme j'en ai maintenant la certitude, je réussis à régler cette affair, il faudra se garer à l'avenir.[11]

Lemieux's interest in Pope's project was sustained following his return to Canada by the reply received to a letter written by him to the British Foreign Secretary to ask "if it could be possible for me to obtain a complete series of the Foreign Office confidential print: 'Correspondence respecting the revision of the treaty of 1894 between Great Britain and Japan,' " as he had "found the record of the British Embassy . . . [in Tokyo] very useful during my negotiations with Count Hayashi, as it contains some important despatches concerning Canada's attitude in the matter." He suggested that the documents be sent directly to Ottawa, and promised that their confidential character would be respected by the Canadian government.[12] This procedure was not new; in 1903 the British government had acceded to Sir Wilfrid Laurier's request "to have four sets of [the Alaska Boundary] correspondence sent over here confidentially for the use of my colleagues and the Counsel who will be concerned in the management of the Canadian end of the business."[13] Indignation in

---

[11] Lemieux to Sir Louis Jetté, Dec. 4, 1907, Lemieux Papers (P.A.C.), 397-398.
[12] Lemieux to Sir Edward Grey, Dec. 13, 1907, *ibid.*, 534.
[13] Laurier to Sir John Anderson, Feb. 18, 1903, Pope Papers, 234.

Ottawa was all the greater, therefore, when the following reply was received from Sir Edward Grey:

I have given my careful consideration to the request which you made. . . .

I am afraid it will not be possible to issue completed volumes of the series owing to the strict rules we are obliged to observe with regard to their distribution and to the principle involved in these rules; but if you will specify what special documents you may wish to have, I will gladly do my best to meet your wishes.[14]

Lemieux sent this letter to Pope for his comments. "I return Sir E. Grey's letter," Pope wrote on February 28, 1908,

which I think calls for no answer. Not merely every volume, but according to my recollections nearly every page of the Confidential Prints, contains some reference to Canada. The series is a whole, and portions of it would be of no use.

What a commentary this affords on our lack of system! If my suggestion had been listened to years ago, we should not have to ask anybody for these papers to-day, for we should have had them ourselves.[15]

Thus the incident served to illustrate the inadequacy of relying henceforth upon Foreign Office sources of information, and emphasized the need for Canada to acquire its own collection of diplomatic documents for the future.

Rodolphe Lemieux became Pope's principal ally within the Cabinet, and the latter sought to keep his enthusiasm for the proposed Department of External Affairs alive and active. Soon after their return from Japan, Pope sent Lemieux a copy of his memorandum of May 25, 1907. "I repeat to you," he remarked in his covering letter,

that if something is not done before long in the way I have suggested, it will be too late. . . . The Foreign Office confidential papers which I obtained for your use in Tokio afford an apt illustration of the system we should have. There is no reason why records of international questions in which we are concerned should not be equally available here, but as you know, not only are they not so available, but there is no attempt made to collect them together. They are scattered through half-a-dozen departments, and a complete record nowhere exists. As I have asked myself over

[14] Grey to Lemieux, Feb. 11, 1908, Lemieux Papers, 888.
[15] Pope to Lemieux, Feb. 24, 1908, *ibid.*, 977.

and over again, how can an official be expected to have a proper acquaintance with these subjects when he cannot even get at the papers that treat
of them?   There ought to be a system under which officials should have
these questions at their fingers' ends, ready whenever they may come up
for adjustment.   At present when an arbitration or anything of the sort
comes on, everything is hurry-skurry, and we start off on our mission with
perhaps half the papers, and that half ill-digested.   Believe me it is a very
important subject and well worth a few hours' consideration on the part
of the Cabinet.[16]

And two days later:

I venture to point out that my suggestion looking towards the establishment
of a special branch of the Public Service to deal with Canada's External
Affairs, is rather a far reaching one, and would involve considerable
reorganization (or organization; for at present there is none) of the method
of conducting our external relations.   It cannot be disposed of simply by
referring a few despatches to this department.   The whole subject will
require to be carefully thought out.   If such a work is to be assigned to this
department, I must have more room and some additional clerks. . . .
What I aim at is the gradual establishment of a sort of Foreign Office.   I
am inclined to think such a scheme might require legislation. . . .[17]

To his supporter within the government, Pope could also add an
even more influential supporter in the person of Earl Grey.   No
Governor-General has taken a more active interest in the affairs of
the nation, and in the policies by which these were directed; none
has so fully exploited the trinity of his prerogatives, to be consulted,
to encourage, and to warn.[18]   As the channel of communication between the Canadian government, the British government and its
Embassy at Washington, Grey became increasingly preoccupied with
the conduct of Canada's external affairs and, towards the end of 1907

---

[16] Feb. 10, 1908, Under Secretary of State: Semi-Official Correspondence, folder
191.
[17] Feb. 12, 1908, Lemieux Papers, 878.
[18] Soon after the new Governor-General's arrival, Pope noted that "Lord Grey
is developing crankish tendencies. . . ."   Pope Diary, entry for May 18, 1905.   By
1909, "when Grey's enthusiasm for proportional representation threatened to become
embarrassing, Laurier 'wished Earl Grey would mind his own business,' and [Mac-
kenzie] King in his diary added: 'The truth is His Ex. is getting into too many
things.' "   R. MacGregor Dawson, William Lyon Mackenzie King: A Political
Biography, Vol. I, 1874-1923 (Toronto, 1958), pp. 174-175.   This propensity probably helps to explain Laurier's refusal, during the latter half of 1908 and early in
1909, to be much moved by Grey's entreaties to act with speed to establish the Department of External Affairs.

and throughout 1908—a period of unprecedented diplomatic activity—increasingly concerned at the confusion attending it. Like Joseph Pope, he attributed much of the confusion to the want of a separate department of government to which would be assigned responsibility for making adequate preparation for negotiations involving Canadian interests. In March 1908 he wrote on this subject to the Colonial Secretary:

Bryce's difficulties in conducting the negotiations [with the United States government] have, I am sorry to say, been increased by the chaotic condition of the Administration here *qua* External Affairs. There is no Department, no official through whose hands all matters dealing with external affairs must go. Consequently there is no record, no continuity, no method, no consistency.

I have represented all this to Laurier, who agrees with every word I say. I regret that he did not, when he came into office 11 years ago, create a Department. Well it is not too late. Do it now, I urge. I fear that must wait until after the Elections, he replies.

I trust I may be able to overcome this fatal procrastination. We have only three men in the Government Service who have any knowledge of details connected with Canada's foreign relations. One drinks at times, the other has a difficulty in expressing his thoughts, and conversation is as difficult as it is to extract an extra tight cork, and the third is the Under Secretary of State, Pope—a really first class official. Not a day should be lost in putting him in charge of a Department of External Affairs under Sir Wilfrid Laurier, and in a short time he would be able to train one or two young men who would take up his work after he has gone. He would have the papers on every question in good shape. Sir W. Laurier's work would be ever so much facilitated, and Canada would be prompt and satisfactory to deal with, instead of the swollen impossible cork, the extraction of which almost bursts a bloodvessel. The results of Bryce's visit will I hope enable me to overcome Laurier's procrastination. There is no one who will benefit from the change more than he will.[19]

The third of Pope's allies was James Bryce, the British Ambassador at Washington. Formally and to a great degree practically responsible for the settlement of Canadian-American differences, Bryce had had ample opportunity for experiencing at first-hand the woefully inadequate facilities that Ottawa provided for the purpose. Too frequently was he on the point of reaching agreement with the

[19] Earl Grey to Lord Elgin, March 28, 1908, Grey Papers, box 14, folder 25.

State Department on some matter of importance to Canada only to discover with concern and chagrin that the Canadian government had changed its stand on the issue, or had allowed it to lie unattended while disposing of other business, or, indeed, had altogether forgotten about it.[20]   After a series of frustrating episodes of this kind he had written to Earl Grey:

All this shows once more the frightful inconvenience of not having in Ottawa a Dept. of External Affairs.   Knowing how Sir Wilfrid is worked . . . I entirely understand his difficulties.   But the loss of time which this constant breaking the chain of negotiations and then trying to rivet the sundered links afresh involves is so great that really nothing seems so urgent as to create at once the needed department.   Will you not continue to press for the doing of this?[21]

It was in fact Bryce who first raised the matter with authorities in the United Kingdom, writing in the first instance to the Colonial Secretary to urge, as Lord Crewe informed Earl Grey, "rather keenly" that a Department of External Affairs be created at Ottawa.   This proposal seems to have been at the outset treated with reserve at Whitehall, perhaps with some apprehension as well.   "It seems to me," Crewe wrote to Earl Grey,

to be a matter requiring no little consideration before it is decided upon. I daresay, as I think I told you before, that the existing arrangements are somewhat haphazard, and may lead to dilatory action, but I should rather

[20] Some measure of the frustrations Bryce encountered in negotiating with the United States on Canada's behalf is provided by the following episode, related by Bryce in a letter dated June 30, 1908, to Earl Grey:
"Your letter of the 22nd June enclosing Minute of P.C. [Privy Council] illustrates admirably the need for an External Affairs Dept. in your Govt.   Laurier suggested to me that instead of 3 arbitrators for the Pecuniary Claims Arbitration we should have two Arbitrators with power to appoint an Umpire when they disagreed.   I conveyed this suggestion unofficially to [Elihu] Root [the United States Secretary of State].   Root accepted it and redrafted the Convention to meet Laurier's view.   Now after all these months [Allen] Aylesworth [the Canadian Minister of Justice] prepares and the P.C. approves a Minute disapproving Root's draft because it embodies Laurier's suggestion!   Aylesworth would seem never to have heard of Laurier's view, tho' I put it into a Memorandum of my talks with Laurier wh. Laurier initialled and approved.   Now where are we?   Are we to tell Root that the P.C. disapproves Laurier's own suggestion which he adopted?"
Grey Papers, box 8, folder W.   A few months later Bryce complained: "The letters and Minutes that come from Canadian Ministers sometimes ignore our communications simply because these have been forgotten, or mislaid, or perhaps never seen by the person who writes to us."   Bryce to Earl Grey, Jan. 7, 1909, *ibid.*, box 9, folder B.
[21] May 11, 1908, *ibid.*, box 8, folder U.

dread the establishment of a regular Foreign Department with a Minister all to itself, which might be likely to undertake or at any rate to attempt independent action in matters upon which we here, and the Foreign Office in particular, ought to have a preliminary word. On the other hand, if it were a question of fitting out the Prime Minister with a small Foreign Bureau containing one or two experienced permanent officials who would give their whole time to these questions and to nothing else, and who would be able to put pressure on the Prime Minister to deal with such matters when they were urgent, instead of postponing them to other matters of domestic interest, I think that nothing but good would result. Perhaps you will think this over and let me know your opinion. Bryce, of course, placed where he is, is naturally disposed to consider the discussion of these international questions the most important work that your Government has to do, but we must not lose sight of the possible danger which I have indicated.[22]

Earl Grey hastened to reassure the British government that nothing so radical as a breach in the diplomatic unity of the Empire would be in prospect as a result of the proposed innovation, and that all that was desired was, as he put it, "that the Prime Minister should have attached to his office a small Department of External Affairs, containing one or two experienced permanent officials, who will give their whole time to External Affairs and nothing else, and who will keep him properly posted."[23] This attempt to minimize the constitutional significance of the project seems to have allayed initial misgiving in London. "The C.O. has been uneasy as to this," wrote Bryce to Earl Grey in August 1908, "lest it should relax the connection with C.O. and F.O., but they now appear to see that it is indispensable, and that in the form not of a separate Ministerial Department but of a secretariat attached to the Prime Minister it need not do any harm."[24]

These representations of Pope, Lemieux, Earl Grey, and Bryce had by this time had their desired effect; henceforth they would be preaching to the converted. "Sir Wilfrid Laurier agrees that [the

---

[22] July 4, 1908, *ibid.*, box 15, folder 29.

[23] Grey to Elgin, July 14, 1908, *ibid.*, box 15, folder 30.

[24] Aug. 10, 1908, *ibid.*, box 8, folder X. The misgivings of the Colonial Office may have reflected to some extent the personality of its Minister. Lord Elgin's tenure, a not kind critic has written, was "undistinguished. His part in conferences on Colonial matters was often said to consist in tugging at his beard in silence, and on one occasion when he was expected to sum up he surprised his colleagues by carefully putting the end of it into his mouth." James Pope-Hennessy, *Lord Crewe: The Likeness of a Liberal* (London, 1956), p. 64.

Department of External Affairs] is needed," Earl Grey wrote on July 14, 1908, "and so do all the members of his Cabinet. Mr. [W. S.] Fielding [the Minister of Finance] has assured me that he will make no objection to finding the money for the additional salaries required."[25] On September 9 Joseph Pope was

told . . . that Sir Wilfrid Laurier had informed the Cabinet of his resolve, immediately after the elections, to erect a Department of External Affairs such as I have long advocated and to place me in charge of it. This the Cabinet unanimously agreed to do. If they really mean this, it is a welcome piece of news. To tell the truth I have been feeling discouraged and disheartened over the apathy with which my suggestions have been received. . . .[26]

2.

"In accordance with your request," Joseph Pope wrote to Laurier on February 6, 1909, "I send you a draft of a proposed Act establishing a Department of *External Affairs*. It is only a first attempt and is no doubt susceptible of improvement, but it may serve as a basis for discussion of the subject."[27] Before Pope's draft became law it underwent a number of modifications, three of which are significant. (1) In Pope's original draft, the Prime Minister is designated as the Minister in charge of the new Department; in the bill in the form to which royal assent was given on May 19, 1909, the Secretary of State is so designated. (2) In Pope's original draft, the Minister in charge of the new Department is to be styled "Secretary of State for External Affairs"; in the bill, the additional function is not made explicit by a new title, and the Minister remains simply the Secretary of State. (3) In Pope's original draft, the Minister in charge of the new Department is described as being responsible for "the *direction* of all matters relating to the external affairs of the Dominion . . ."; in the bill, for "the *conduct* of all official communications . . ."; while in Pope's proposed but unimplemented revisions of the bill, "those I thought of suggesting in anticipation of the changes the Bill was undergoing but [which] I never had a chance to press,"[28] for "the *supervision* of all matters in connection with the external affairs of

[25] Grey Papers, box 15, folder 30.
[26] Pope Diary, entry for Sept. 9, 1909.
[27] Under Secretary of State: Semi-Official Correspondence, folder 375.
[28] *Ibid.*

Canada . . ." (author's italics). Each of these discrepancies requires further examination.

The provision in the Act placing the new Department under the Secretary of State, Pope wrote in his diary on March 4, 1909, was "a *great* mistake. It should be under the Prime Minister."[29] Similar views had been expressed that day in the House of Commons by Conservative critics. "You have a more simple, economical and thorough manner of dealing with this matter," George Foster had declared, "if you attach a little body of expert clerks to the Privy Council, put them under the Prime Minister, where, I think, these things ought to be, and let them do all this work of keeping the records. . . ."[30] "If we are to concede what the Prime Minister has argued for," remarked R. L. Borden, ". . . then I say that that department should be under the control of the Prime Minister and not under the control of the Secretary of State"; and he cited the Australian precedent in support of this contention.[31] Just why the new Department was placed under the Secretary of State remains obscure. In debate, Laurier brushed the criticism aside. "It does not matter," he insisted, "under which minister the Department of External Affairs may be placed. . . ."[32] Pope later wrote that his original draft of the bill in this respect "was changed at the last moment" for "some reason of which I am ignorant." He pointed out, however, that despite the Act's assignment of responsibility to the Secretary of State, it was Laurier as Prime Minister rather than Charles Murphy as Secretary of State upon whom the burden of the new Department fell. "Sir Wilfrid Laurier even in the beginning," Pope pointed out in a memorandum written for Borden in 1912,

was so impressed with the necessity for having supervision over the Department that he added to the draft Minute of Council a provision that a duplicate of all despatches should be sent to him.

All important subjects of negotiation were . . . laid by me before the Prime Minister, according to Sir Wilfrid's instructions. He discussed them with

[29] Pope Diary, entry for March 4, 1909.
[30] Canada, *House of Commons Debates*, 1909, I, March 4, col. 1988.
[31] *Ibid.*, col. 2002. "The resignation of Alfred Deakin's second administration in November 1908 marks the last occasion when the original [Australian] Department of External Affairs had the prime minister as its head. Thus, when Robert Borden, in the Canadian House of Commons in 1909, referred to Australian precedent as a justification for attaching the projected Canadian external affairs portfolio to the office of prime minister, he was in error . . . ." MacKirdy, *op. cit.*, p. 505.
[32] Canada, *H. of C. Debates*, 1909, I, col. 2003.

me, and when he had decided on a line of action (which might or might not be in accordance with the view of the Department immediately concerned, or perhaps before the despatch had reached that Department) I would, after acquainting that Department with the Prime Minister's wishes, prepare a report to be signed—not however by the Prime Minister, but by the Secretary of State, whose first knowledge of the subject was thus a cut and dried report set before him to sign."[33]

Following the defeat of the Laurier Government in 1911, Earl Grey wrote to James Bryce that he had already told Borden "that I think it is imperative in the interests of the Crown that the External Affairs Department should be removed from the Secretary of State's Department to his own."[34] At this time of transferring power there seems to have been some talk of placing the Department under the President of the Privy Council. If, as was ordinarily the case, the Prime Minister was also President of the Privy Council, the result desired by Pope and Grey would be achieved. But, as Pope promptly pointed out to Borden,

of your seven predecessors in the office of Prime Minister, three never held the office of President of the Privy Council when Premier, and a fourth was successively Minister of Justice, Interior and Railways. To transfer the External Affairs from one portfolio to another, would not tend to its prestige or importance. I still venture to hope that you may see your way to take this office under you as Prime Minister.[35]

Borden, who in the 1909 debate on the Act to create the Department of External Affairs had urged that the Prime Minister be placed in charge, was easily convinced by Pope's arguments. Accordingly, on April 15, 1912, assent was given to "An Act respecting the Department of External Affairs," of which the second and third paragraphs read as follows:

2. There shall be a Department of the Government of Canada to be called the Department of External Affairs, over which the Secretary of State for External Affairs shall preside.

3. The Member of the King's Privy Council for Canada holding the recognized position of First Minister shall be the Secretary of State for External Affairs. . . .[36]

[33] Jan. 10, 1912, Borden Papers (P.A.C.), OC 552.
[34] Sept. 26, 1911, Grey Papers, box 11, folder D.
[35] Dec. 30, 1911, Borden Papers, OC 552.
[36] 2 George V, c. 22.

As his original draft of the Act of 1909 makes clear, it had been Pope's intention that the Minister in charge of the new Department should receive the title "Secretary of State for External Affairs." But the Act placed the Department under the Secretary of State, creating no new portfolio with which the bearer of the additional responsibility might be invested, even though it had created the position of an Under Secretary of State for External Affairs. This anomaly irritated Pope's sensibilities. "Does not the existing statute," he wrote to Borden,

in creating the office of "Under-Secretary of State for External Affairs", appear to contemplate that there shall be a Secretary of State for External Affairs? I do not quite see how there could be an Under-Secretary of State for External Affairs without a Secretary of State for External Affairs, but if there were, such official would popularly be regarded as in some sense amenable to the jurisdiction, not merely of *the* Secretary of State, but also (as is more or less the case at the present moment) of the officer at present known as "*the* Under Secretary of State":

The existence of two Secretaries of State, one for *Home*, the other for *External* affairs is so reasonable in itself and so accordant with British usage that I feel it would speedily commend itself to public opinion, in so far as public opinion has any interest in such matters.[37]

Moreover, despite the perverse wording of the Act of 1909, the Secretary of State, acting in his capacity as the Minister in charge of the new Department, had been directed by none other than the Prime Minister to use the title which Pope had originally suggested. "The first recommendation I laid before him [Laurier]," Pope wrote to Borden, "was prepared for signature as 'Secretary of State.' Without any suggestions on my part he added, with his own hand, the words 'for External Affairs' and directed that that title should be always used."[38] This direction was duly carried out, for the diplomatic correspondence of the period 1909-1911 bearing the signature of Charles Murphy describes him as "Secretary of State for External Affairs," an office not recognized by law until the Act of 1912 removed the anomaly, greatly to Pope's satisfaction.

No part of the legislation creating the Department of External Affairs caused as much controversy at the time of its enactment as its third paragraph. "I do not like the expression: 'shall have the con-

[37] Dec. 30, 1911, Borden Papers, OC 552.
[38] Jan. 10, 1912, *ibid.*

duct of all official communications between the Government of Canada and the Government of any other country,'" Pope wrote to W. H. Walker[39] on March 10, 1909:

That would rather imply that the Government of Canada can conduct direct negotiations. It is quite evident from the Prime Minister's speech [in the House of Commons on March 4] and that of Mr. Murphy, that they do not mean this. It is just a bit of clumsy drafting. Can you think of any qualifying phrase that might be inserted, such for example as, after the word "communications", "through the usual channel", or something of that sort?[40]

Walker replied:

I cannot bring myself to interpret the phrase "conduct of communications", even if qualified as you suggest, to mean anything else than an actual carrying on of correspondence by the Secretary of State.

Personally I am not prepared to criticize the policy involved in such an interpretation. It might be supported on grounds of constitutional theory as well as of convenience; and possibly might be sanctioned by H.M. Government.

But assuming that this is not the Government's policy it seems to me that the language of the Bill might be brought more into harmony with what I believe is your own view, and the view which I understand Sir Wilfrid to advance in his explanation, by substituting "direction" or "superintendence" for "conduct". I can quite see that neither substitution is altogether satisfactory, for, in view of the procedure now followed, according to which his Exc ᵛ· actually makes the communications, both are open to the objection of implying an inversion of the relative positions of Governor and Minister and a control exercised over the former by the latter.[41]

The Governor-General himself was quick to sense and to attempt to forestall the possibility that the wording of the Act might weaken the authority of his office. "His Excellency is much worked up over the wording of the External Affairs Bill as brought down," Pope wrote on March 12, "particularly Sect. 3. . . . I merely said that in the circumstances I could not do anything, and that His Excellency ought

---

[39] W. H. Walker, a graduate of the University of Toronto and Osgoode Hall, served in the Governor-General's office before entering the Department of External Affairs in June 1909. He became Assistant Under Secretary in 1911, remaining in that post until his death in 1933.

[40] Under Secretary of State: Semi-Official Correspondence, folder 375.

[41] March 12, 1909, *ibid.*

to see his Ministers on the point."[42] Promptly Earl Grey did so, and wrote on May 3 to Lord Crewe of the result:

I called the attention of Sir Wilfrid as soon as it was drafted to the fact that the word "conduct" in clause 3 did not correctly interpret the speeches made by himself and Mr. Aylesworth in the debate on the introduction of the Bill: that to give the Secretary of State the "conduct" of official communications between the Government of Canada and other Governments, would be regarded as an improper attempt to shelve the Governor General; that I was aware that this was not his intention, and that the substitution of the word "care" for the word "conduct" was all that was required. He unreservedly agreed with all I said, and undertook that the word "care" should be substituted. Although he made a note at my request in his pocket book, he must have forgotten to give any instructions in the matter, with the result that the bill has passed the Commons and the second reading of the Senate in its unamended form.

I saw the Secretary of State [Murphy], Sir Wilfrid Laurier and the Minister of Justice [Aylesworth] this morning and pointed out to them the importance of amending the bill in this direction in Committee of the Senate. They all three promised that it should be done, so I hope that matter is all right. If Sir Wilfrid Laurier had allowed this bill to be passed in its original form I should have had to request him to bring in an amending act, in order to avoid men of the Ewart stamp from . . . deducing from it that the Governor General was a superfluous and unnecessary official.[43]

Whatever promise Laurier may have made to amend the bill in the manner desired by the Governor-General, he did not keep it. The bill became law, and the Minister of the new Department became responsible for the "conduct" rather than the "care" of diplomatic correspondence. Grey was still determined that the offending phrase should not affect his position as the channel of communication with the governments of other countries. He wrote to the British Ambassador at Washington:

There is no reason why you should not at once start a correspondence with the External Affairs Department, but with the view of preventing the office of Governor General drifting into a subordinate and undignified position, I must ask you to send me, for purposes of filing in my office, copies of any private communications you may send to the Secretary of the

[42] Pope Diary, entry for March 12, 1909.
[43] May 3, 1909, Grey Papers, box 15, folder 36.

Department for External Affairs; and on my return from England I think it would be as well if the correspondence went as much as possible through the Governor General, in order that he should know exactly how things are moving. Apart from the principle involved it should often be in the power of the Governor General to help matters forward by private non-official talks with men like the Chief Justice or other members of the Cabinet, besides the Prime Minister.[44]

Bryce replied:

With all you say about the new External Affairs Department I agree. It was my own feeling that the Embassy ought to correspond with you, not with the 'External Affairs', not merely because that is the proper constitutional course but also because it is the course most likely to advance business and to secure impartial interests. The Governor General ought to know all that is passing. The Ambassador can say things to him he would not say equally well to the Prime Minister and can consider with him the general Imperial bearings of what is passing. . . . Sometimes it may be well for the Embassy to jog the memory of the Cabinet through "External Affairs", sometimes to ask External Affairs what is passing—but the really important correspondence ought in my view as in yours to be, still and always, with the Governor General.[45]

"Still and always" proved in fact to mean the two remaining years of Earl Grey's governor-generalship. By 1912 the office of his successor, the Duke of Connaught, informed the British Embassy at Washington of its view that "to prevent direct correspondence between the Embassy and the First Minister . . . would be as impossible to do as it would be undesirable."[46] But Grey never lost hope. As late as 1910 he was still asking Laurier to amend the Act. The Prime Minister did not do so, possibly because he had been impressed by Charles Murphy's argument that as the new Department was "not popular with some of my colleagues, and still less so with many of the Government supporters," it was well to avoid "attracting the attention of Council or Parliament to unimportant details that are sure to excite opposition and suspicion." An equally plausible explanation is that by this time Laurier had become wholly impatient with Grey's persistent intrusions into government policy. In any event, as Murphy did not fail to point out, "Earl Grey will be leaving Canada in

---

[44] Grey to Bryce, June 2, 1909, *ibid.*, box 9, folder R.
[45] June 10, 1909, *ibid.*
[46] Col. Henry C. Lowther to Eustace Percy, March 13, 1912, Borden Papers, OC 39.

a couple of months, the matter is not one with which he is particularly concerned and his successor will never dream of raising such an objection."[47]   This prediction proved wholly correct.

3.

The Act creating the new Department of government could not as easily bring into being its physical requirements.   "I am in the most extraordinary position," wrote Joseph Pope on the fourth day of his new career, "—a deputy head without an office or a staff."[48]   The battle for clerical assistance was immediately begun.   "We are starting a Department with nothing," Pope wrote to his Minister.   "We have to design books, forms, and in fact to think out a whole system in detail,"[49] and for this purpose he requested two "typewriters" (typists), duly though temporarily acquired.   During the first few weeks Pope not only remained in his old office but was required to share it with the official succeeding to his duties as Under Secretary of State.   He presented at this time a somewhat pathetic spectacle. "Mr. Pope," Earl Grey wrote to James Bryce, "has not even a table to write on, or a chair to sit in; no cupboards in which to put his papers and his books, and as he is a gentleman who moves with dignity and deliberation some time must elapse to enable him to settle down comfortably in the midst of his new surroundings."[50]   During the summer of 1909 he occupied some vacant rooms in the House of Commons, but the return of the legislators forced another evacuation.   Space above a barber shop in Bank Street was all that could be found, and it was here that Grey, returning to Ottawa in October after a trip to the Canadian West, discovered to his "great disappointment"[51] the entire staff of a branch of government to which Laurier had promised to attach "the dignity and importance of a department by itself."[52]   There were thus extenuating circumstances for the complaint a year later by the British Ambassador at Washington that its creation "has not, so far, accelerated business."[53]

[47] Murphy to Laurier, April 22, 1910, Laurier Papers, 170261-2.
[48] Pope Diary, entry for June 4, 1909.
[49] Pope to Murphy, June 30, 1909, Murphy Papers (P.A.C.).
[50] June 2, 1909, Grey Papers, box 9, folder R.
[51] Grey to Laurier, Nov. 3, 1909, Laurier Papers, 206367-9.
[52] Canada, H. of C. Debates, session 1909, I, March 4, col. 2004.
[53] Bryce to Grey, July 4, 1910, Grey Papers, box 10, folder Q.

Amidst all the confusion the work of the new Department was begun. A necessary first step was to cast about for some principles of organization. In 1898 Pope had visited the Department of State at Washington "with a view of examining into their system of keeping their records," and while he noted approvingly that these "run back to 1789 and nothing is ever destroyed," he was not impressed by its method. "They do not have all the papers relating to a certain case together, but have to hunt them up separately, which to my mind is quite a disadvantage."[54]   In 1909 a study was made of the Australian Department of External Affairs, but this also failed to provide a useful model. "Their Department seems to have a much wider sphere of activity than is contemplated for the Canadian one," wrote W. H. Walker, "and while the information supplied is interesting so far as it goes it does not seem to me very helpful towards establishing an organization or procedure for the new Depart[t]."[55]   It was accordingly to the Foreign Office that the Canadian government eventually turned. In 1910 Laurier decided to send Pope to London "to look into the Foreign Office system and to collect back records," wishing, as Pope noted in his diary, "the foundations well and truly laid."[56]   Armed with letters of introduction to Sir Edward Grey and Lord Crewe, Pope arrived at Whitehall, where, he reported to Laurier, he found "every facility afforded me."[57]   This assignment, like the one following—"the periodical issue of a series of Canadian State Papers"[58]—was a labor which the new permanent head found the most congenial and satisfying of his office. A more dramatic impact on events he "neither claimed nor desired."[59]   Such larger ambitions were left to his successors. Pope's own lasting achievement lay less in his influence upon foreign policy (though that was greater than is sometimes supposed) than in the creation of the Department which in the fifth decade of its history was to do so much to raise Canada from the rank of a small country to that of a Middle Power.

[54] Pope Diary, entry for Dec. 6, 1898.
[55] Walker to Pope, May 13, 1909, Under Secretary of State: Semi-Official Correspondence, folder 375.
[56] Pope Diary, entry for Jan. 16, 1910.
[57] Laurier Papers, 170643-52.
[58] Pope to H. P. Biggar, Oct. 25, 1910, Under Secretary of State: Semi-Official Correspondence, box 39.
[59] Soward, op. cit., p. 8.

Canadian External Affairs During World War I

Gaddis Smith

It has long been recognized that the Great War of 1914-1918 permanently and profoundly altered Canada's attitude towards external affairs and her position in the world. As one historian has written, with pardonable oversimplification, "Canada entered the war a colony, she emerged from it close to an independent state."[1] Despite the acknowledged importance of the war, however, comparatively little has been written about the crucial details of Canada's wartime experience. This is especially so in the realm of the external affairs of the Canadian government. Although some attention has been given to such constitutional developments as the formation of the Imperial War Cabinets of 1917 and 1918 and the acquisition of separate Dominion representation at the Paris Peace Conference, almost nothing has been written concerning the specific day-by-day problems in external affairs faced by Canada during the war.

This paper is a brief attempt to explain through an examination of those day-by-day problems how Canadian external policies grew between 1914 and 1918. The focus, therefore, is less on "status" and "nationhood" in the abstract and more on practical expedients adopted to meet specific situations; less on the much publicized constitutional pronouncements of the time and more on problems of trade, transportation, and industrial growth.

[1] Arthur R. M. Lower, *Colony to Nation: A History of Canada* (Toronto, 1946), p. 470.

1. The Outbreak of War

On the eve of World War I Canadian interest in matters of external affairs was a fluctuating thing, one moment swelling on a flood of controversy; the next moment falling back to indifference. By July 1914 the most recent controversy, the Senate-obstructed proposal that Canada pay for the building of three dreadnoughts for the British Navy, had subsided.[2] It was vacation time and external policy was a matter of slight public or government concern.

Equally slight in 1914 was the machinery for the conduct of external policy. The five-year old Department of External Affairs, over a barbershop on Ottawa's Bank Street, was little more than a filing bureau without responsibility for policy.[3] There the Under Secretary of the Department, meticulous and old-fashioned Sir Joseph Pope, kept every chit of paper precisely in place, watched over the typists, and in the evening peddled sedately home on his bicycle. Abroad the Dominion was represented by the timid but conscientious Sir George H. Perley, who was acting temporarily as High Commissioner in London following the death of the superannuated Lord Strathcona. In addition a band of sixteen trade commissioners, concentrated in Western Europe, worked to build Canada's trade.[4] In Washington there was no Canadian representative of any sort, although issues with the United States could be handled—depending on their nature and importance—by the British Ambassador in Washington (Sir Cecil Spring-Rice), the new International Joint Commission, or by members of the Canadian government traveling south on an *ad hoc* basis.[5] Information on external conditions came to the government mostly from the newspapers, occasionally from the British Colonial Office and the British Embassy in Washington

[2] Gilbert Norman Tucker, *The Naval Service of Canada* (Ottawa, 1952), I, 170-211, surveys the dreadnought issue from conception to miscarriage.

[3] F. H. Soward has provided a succinct account of *The Department of External Affairs and Canadian Autonomy, 1899-1939*, Canadian Historical Association Booklet No. 7 (Ottawa, 1956), while James Eayrs has gone into great detail in presenting "The Origins of Canada's Department of External Affairs," Chapter 1 of this volume.

[4] H. Gordon Skilling, *Canadian Representation Abroad* (Toronto, 1945), pp. 51-52. The chapter "Building Canada's Trade" is also especially useful.

[5] John S. Galbraith, *The Establishment of Canadian Diplomatic Status at Washington* (Berkeley and Los Angeles, 1951) is a good discussion of its subject but incomplete for the period of World War I. Chirakaikaran Joseph Chacko, *The International Joint Commission: Between the United States of America and the Dominion of Canada* (New York, 1932) is workmanlike.

which forwarded bland despatches to the Governor-General, and most usefully from private individuals close to members of the government. Decisions, when any were needed, were made almost exclusively by Prime Minister Sir Robert Borden, who by virtue of his office was also Secretary of State for External Affairs. For peace-time such arrangements worked well enough.

But then came war. Ominous headlines proclaimed the emergency. Sir Robert Borden broke off a holiday and rushed back to Ottawa. Without hesitation he cabled the British government on August 1, 1914, that Canada would "make every sacrifice necessary" if Great Britain became involved in war.[6] That Canada might not go to war was unthinkable. August 4 at midnight the deadline passed on Great Britain's ultimatum to Germany. The British Empire was at war.

Although eventual war had long been anticipated, the Canadian government had devoted little forethought to the policies a crisis might require. Details of administrative procedure for alerting government departments at the outbreak of war had been devised by a committee working since January 1914 and headed by Sir Joseph Pope, but that was all. The general image of what the war would be like was uncomplicated; it would be short and as far as the British Empire was concerned would doubtless be fought cleanly and dramatically with the invincible dreadnought fleet. Canada, of course, would prepare an overseas contingent, perhaps twenty thousand men, and might be of some slight economic assistance. From London Sir George Perley suggested a gift to Great Britain of a "million or two barrels of flour," a move that would be popular in the Canadian West. It was pleasant to be able to combine politics and patriotism. A million bags of flour were offered and accepted.[7]

A few days of war dispelled all dreams of simplicity. All was rush and confusion in Ottawa, confusion made worse by the almost total lack of precise information about what was happening in Europe. As a prominent member of the Cabinet noted in his diary, he and his colleagues were beset by a "feverish condition of expectancy and uncertainty and ignorance of what is developing behind the scenes and how it will affect the fate of the nations." In Cabinet meetings

[6] Henry Borden, ed., *Robert Laird Borden: His Memoirs* (Toronto, 1938), I, 450-452.
[7] Perley to Borden, Aug. 3, 1914, Papers of Sir George Perley, Public Archives of Canada, Ottawa, box 1; see also Borden, *Memoirs*, I, 457.

discussions seemed to lack all consistency.[8] Such a situation was
scarcely conducive to any consideration of the larger conditions and
objectives of the war. The Canadian government more than had its
hands full with the details of raising the first contingent for overseas
and with meeting, as best it could, the commercial and financial
dislocations brought about by the war.

And yet in the opening days of war there was one brief excursion
into high policy. It dealt with the entry of Japan into the war and,
although an isolated incident, well illustrates Canada's then informal
manner of conducting external affairs. It also has an incidental
significance for the postwar future. The British government had
asked on August 7 for Japan's aid against German armed vessels in
Chinese waters.[9] Four days later the British told the Canadian
government that a Japanese declaration of war against Germany was
imminent.[10] Sir Robert Bordon felt that no Canadian comment was
necessary, but not so Premier Sir Richard McBride of British Columbia. McBride was distraught. Sharing the distrust of Japan common
to the Pacific coast of Canada and the United States, he felt that the
Japanese must be kept out of the war.[11] Accordingly McBride sent
a telegram to Borden, who in turn relayed the alarmed message to
First Lord of the Admiralty Winston Churchill. Japan would not
hesitate to betray Great Britain and co-operate with Germany, warned
McBride. The Anglo-Japanese alliance would make no difference.[12]
Churchill replied immediately that there was no need for alarm.
Japan "must be welcome as a comrade and an ally. . . . Tell McBride
we are sending two powerful British cruisers to Pacific coast. Please
reassure him privately. Any declaration against entry of Japan into
war would do harm."[13]

Meanwhile Sir Edward Grey, in order to calm apprehensions in
Canada and the United States as well as in Australia and New Zealand, was trying to get Japan to promise explicitly to limit her area

[8] Diary of Sir George Foster (Minister of Trade and Commerce), Aug. 14, 1914,
Papers of Sir George Foster, Public Archives of Canada.
[9] Charles Nelson Spinks has described "Japan's Entrance into the World War,"
Pacific Historical Review, V (1936), 297-311.
[10] Colonial Secretary to the Governor-General, Aug. 11, 1914, Papers of Sir
Robert Borden, Public Archives of Canada, box 287.
[11] The efforts of the American government during these same days to keep Japan
neutral have been traced by Ernest R. May, "American Policy and Japan's Entrance
into World War I," *Mississippi Valley Historical Review*, XL (Sept. 1953), 279-290.
[12] Borden to Churchill, Aug. 13, 1914, Borden Papers, file OC 231.
[13] Churchill to Borden, Aug. 14, 1914, *ibid.*

of operations to the China Sea and to an attack on the German base at Kiaochow.[14] This the Japanese would not promise, and on August 15 delivered the war ultimatum, without geographical limitations, to Germany. No more on the subject was heard from Canada.

The Canadian government, putting worries over international diplomacy and the alignment of powers aside for the time being, turned full attention to preparing the war economy and organizing an armed force. Seemingly these were domestic matters, but quickly they became enmeshed in problems of external policy. How could the government work to overcome the competition of the neutral United States as a producer of war materials for the Allies? How could the British be encouraged to send those orders to Canada which would simultaneously stimulate the growth of Canadian industry in variety and volume, protect the Canadian government from domestic political unrest arising from economic causes, and best further the over-all war effort? On the military level, how could Canada's overseas forces be intelligently directed in the national interest while locked of necessity in the agonizing life-wasting pattern of trench warfare over which even the British and French high commands had so little control?

These questions and others like them fed the watershed of Canadian wartime policy. Flowing from them were secondary questions. How could outmoded institutions and procedures be swept away? How could the Canadian government obtain the vital information deemed necessary for the direction of policy? How could Canada develop a new and more direct diplomatic relationship with the United States? Only when the daily pressure lessened and the moment of victory approached was there time to consider more permanent questions. What position should Canada have among nations? What relation should Canadian external policy have to the foreign policies of Great Britain and the United States? More specifically, what should Canada's attitude be towards a Bolshevik Russia, towards a defeated Germany, towards the general nature of the peace settlement?

2. Wartime Economic Diplomacy

Government effort to encourage the growth of the Canadian economy, with the emphasis on industry (the heavier the better), is

[14] Spinks, *op. cit.*, p. 308.

a major theme in Canadian history. During World War I it was also a major theme in Canadian diplomacy, at times becoming an obsession nearly blotting out all other considerations of external policy.

The single most pressing problem for the Canadian government during the first seven months of 1914 was the unhealthy state of the economy. A depression had settled over Canada, a depression which seemed particularly acute and discouraging because it followed the greatest boom in the country's history. The immediate impact of the outbreak of the war was to make the depression worse. As a result, the first period of the government's wartime external policy became primarily a scramble after business, an effort to take advantage of the war as a means of wiping out unemployment and of bringing prosperity back to Canada.

In the opening months of the war before Canadian troops were being wounded and killed, industrial opinion greeted the crisis with open jubilation. "Rich prizes for Canadian Manufacturers" headlined the monthly journal of the Canadian Manufacturers' Association in September as it gleefully presented a statistical analysis of the German trade which Canada could easily capture.[15] That autumn the C.M.A. launched its strident, well-financed "Made in Canada" campaign. Even the voice of the prairies was caught up in the spirit of the times. In September the *Manitoba Free Press* began a series of ten articles on the general subject of "Industrial Canada's Opportunity to Secure Millions in Trade Abandoned by European Countries at War."[16] Nearly every newspaper reflected the same optimism.

Hopes of an immediate boom in general trade not surprisingly proved unfounded, and it soon became apparent that if Canadian industry was to prosper it would have to do so by producing the implements and supplies of war. But instead of seeing orders pour in, Canadian manufacturers, with plants shut down or running part time, read in the newspapers of huge British and French orders being placed in the United States. Unemployment, only partially relieved by army recruiting, became an ever more serious problem. At Sydney Mines, Nova Scotia, reported a correspondent of the *Labour Gazette*, the steel plant was "closed down completely and men and officials were paid off." In Toronto "the labour situation . . . entered

[15] *Industrial Canada*, Sept. 1914.
[16] *Manitoba Free Press* (Winnipeg), Sept. 15, 1914.

upon a more serious phase than at any previous time . . . . The British Welcome League building [receiving center for immigrants], recently closed, will be used during the coming season to accommodate the unemployed."[17] From every center in Canada came similar dark reports.

And into Ottawa flowed a stream of complaints. Could not the government do something? Could not Canada receive a greater share of war orders? As seen by the Prime Minister the situation was grave, and required vigorous protests to the British government. Cabling to Perley, who was instructed to make the necessary representations in London, Borden minced no words:

Not only the people of Canada as a whole but individuals are making sacrifices undreamed of to support Empire in this war. A very painful and even bitter feeling is being aroused throughout the Dominion. Men are going without bread in Canada while those across the line are receiving wages for work that could be done as efficiently and as cheaply in this country. You cannot emphasize too strongly the consideration set forth in this message. Public opinion is being seriously aroused as to most gravely affect our future action.[18]

The implications were clear. Canada could not wage war with a faltering economy. If the needed stimulus did not come, the reaction of embittered public opinion conceivably could force reconsideration of the nature and extent of Canada's participation in the war.

As the months went by conditions did not seem to improve. In the United States, President Woodrow Wilson had reversed the original ban on loans to the belligerent government largely on the argument of State Department Counselor Robert Lansing that "otherwise the buying power of these foreign purchasers will dry up and the business will go to Australia, Canada, Argentine and elsewhere. . . . we will have neglected our foreign trade at the time of our . . . greatest opportunity."[19] This, of course, was no help to Canada.

Item by item throughout the winter and spring of 1915 the Canadian government stressed the available or easily developed facilities in Canada for war production. No other subject was dealt with as extensively by the government in its messages sent abroad. By far the most important industry was munitions, and here Canada

---

[17] *Labour Gazette*, XV (Sept. 1914), 339, 359.

[18] Borden to Perley, Nov. 27, 1914, Perley Papers, box 2.

[19] United States Department of State, *Papers Relating to the Foreign Relations of the United States: The Lansing Papers, 1914-1920* (Washington, 1939), I, 139.

labored under a special burden: the Shell Committee. This was an organization set up early in 1915 by Sir Sam Hughes, the flamboyant and unbalanced Minister of Militia and Defence, to control all munitions production. The Committee gave the appearance of great energy but was wasteful, inefficient, suspected of corruption, and—worst of all—thoroughly distrusted by the British government.

Despite such handicaps production slowly increased, but not fast enough to eliminate unemployment or to check mounting irritation at the apparent continued preference of Great Britain for the United States over Canada as a source of supply. The political opposition seized the chance to slash at the Borden Government, whose position was none too strong. The Liberal Edmonton *Bulletin*, for example, effectively if unfairly denounced the government for inaction: "It is easier to pile on war taxes than it is to rustle business for the country."[20] In Parliament, where informed discussion of external affairs was notoriously infrequent, the problem of war orders was one of the few subjects of an external nature to be debated during the war. Thus, Perley was criticized as being a poor and unbusinesslike High Commissioner who had not done enough to "sell" Canada. "If Canada's facilities had been brought to the attention of the British Government," said E. M. Macdonald, a vociferous Liberal M.P., "millions of dollars that have gone to the United States would have been spent in Canada."[21] The government, in fact, had done little else but advertise Canada's facilities, but the criticism nevertheless struck a sore point.

From the point of view of the ardent Canadian imperialist the signs were especially ominous. One Conservative politico in Ottawa reported to the influential Sir John Willison, editor of the Toronto *News* and Canadian correspondent of the *Times* (London), that daily he saw letters with such phrases as: "When Britain wants men she comes to Canada; when she wants goods she goes to the United States. . . . If Canada ceased sending men she might have a chance to sell Britain some war supplies. . . . It doesn't pay Canada to be British."[22] Willison sent a copy of the letter to the editor of the

---

[20] Edmonton *Bulletin*, May 10, 1915.

[21] Canada, House of Commons, *Debates*, 1916, II (Feb. 21, 1916), 959.

[22] T. H. Blacklock to Willison, July 20, 1915, Papers of Sir John Willison, Public Archives of Canada, Ottawa, folder 309.

Times and stressed the plea: "Could you not through the *Times* sound a warning to Britain?"[23]

Extravagant and overwrought as were these alarming sentiments, they still had to be taken into account. Therefore, in the summer of 1915 Borden gave up on correspondence and made the first of four wartime trips to Great Britain. His mission had two purposes: first, to present in person Canada's claims for war orders in preference over the United States; and second, to gain a systematic understanding of British war policy in order that he in turn could direct Canada's efforts more intelligently. In both respects his mission was a failure. After six weeks of going "from pillar to post, from one member of the British Government to another," he knew little more than when he left Canada. Finally on the eve of his return he went in desperation to the Colonial Secretary, at that time Bonar Law, and said bluntly:

Unless I obtain this reasonable information which is due to me as Prime Minister of Canada, I shall not advise my countrymen to put further effort into the winning of the War. In three days time I am leaving and now I come to you for the purpose of conveying through you to the British Government the decision I have just announced.[24]

A hurried conference was arranged with Lloyd George, then Minister of Munitions and the dynamo of the otherwise enervated coalition government. It is significant that Prime Minister Herbert Asquith was by-passed, for Asquith showed little interest in Canada's point of view or special problems. This conference in gloomy circumstances was the beginning of a Borden-Lloyd George *rapport* which was to grow steadily until 1919 and which is an important element in Canada's wartime history. As they talked the two men reinforced each other's opinions about the weakness of Britain's war effort, but when the conversation was over Borden had put aside his threat to withdraw Canada's support.

Borden's 1915 trip marked the low point. Back in Canada in the autumn of 1915 the pulse of industry began to quicken. In December the hopeless Shell Committee was replaced under an agreement reached after Borden's trip, by the Imperial Munitions Board, an agency of the British—not the Canadian—government. The board, whose chairman was the Toronto pork-packing magnate Sir Joseph Flavelle, was staffed by Englishmen as well as Canadians and was directly responsible to the British Minister of Munitions. Its achievements were prodigious. It effectively organized the mushrooming munitions industry, distributed orders with political acumen among the provinces, and attracted to Canada all the business factories could handle. In three years the board shipped sixty million artillery shells from Canada, some as large as nine inches; produced in its own factory close to three thousand airplanes; and played a key role in creating a large shipbuilding industry by the end of the war. In all the board spent $1,250,000,000.

The fact that this British government board was created to run the core of the Canadian economy contradicts the theory that Canada moved in a straight line during the war "from colony to nation." Indeed, the board was vigorously attacked at the time by the nationhood flagwavers as an intolerable curtailment of Canadian autonomy and as evidence of abject servility on the part of Borden and his Government. Admittedly the board diminished Canada's "status" but it developed the country's industry. For that reason Borden welcomed the board's formation, gave it every possible encouragement and support, and never uttered a word of criticism. The Imperial Munitions Board is the best illustration of the fact that "nationhood" in the abstract was not a goal of external policy during the war but was rather a means to be used or denied as the occasion demanded.[25]

Even with the end of unemployment the pressure to "rustle business" remained. In Parliament the subject remained prominent. "We have nothing to gain from the war as far as territory or wealth is concerned," said Colonel J. A. Currie, an M.P. who had returned from heavy fighting in France. "The only thing we can possibly get out of the war is trade. I do not say that a war should be waged for the purposes of trade, but we all know that even although the

[25] The voluminous papers of Sir Joseph Flavelle in the Public Archives of Canada, Ottawa, reveal the workings of this enormous undertaking. David Carnegie, *The History of Munitions Supply in Canada, 1914-1918* (Toronto, 1925) is useful but does not deal with the all-important political aspects of the board's activities. Colonel Carnegie was a member of both the old Shell Committee and the board. It is noteworthy that Borden studiously avoided discussing the Imperial Munitions Board in his *Memoirs*.

eagle soars very high, still he has to come down to the hedges to get a living. It is the same with the country."[26]

Meanwhile, the government with the aid of the Imperial Munitions Board kept on advertising Canadian industry through every channel and lost no opportunities to attract non-British customers, Russia being the prime target. The Department of Trade and Commerce in 1915 and 1916 sent two commissioners to Russia.[27] The Imperial Munitions Board also sent a mission which convinced the Tsarist government to establish a Russian Purchasing Commission in Ottawa. This was done and substantial orders were obtained, with more promised. But unfortunately "the Russian Revolution and the subsequent withdrawal of Russia from the War, led to the stoppage of Russian supplies, before the operations of the Commission had assumed any importance."[28] Here was yet another incidental repercussion of that momentous revolution.

Although business was booming, one intractable problem remained: ocean transportation. There simply was not enough shipping in the world to handle British needs and keep ahead of the ravages of the German submarines. In order to meet the desperate shortage the British Admiralty embarked on a wholesale program of requisitioning ships. Much tonnage was withdrawn from the Canadian coastal, Lakes, and transatlantic and transpacific shipping lanes. Many of these withdrawals were considered by the Canadian government to strike at vital national interests. What was the solution to this conflict? There was none—except to engage in interminable, inconclusive, and usually acrimonious diplomacy.

The winter of 1916, to give one example, was filled with a diplomatic tug of war over four colliers under charter to the Dominion Coal Company. We must have those ships, said the Admiralty. If the colliers go, said the company and the Canadian government, the coal mines will shut down, thousands will be unemployed, homes will go unheated, scores of factories will come to a halt. The Admiralty answered that such factors could not be considered, and even went so far as to charge the Dominion Coal Company with being "disloyal."[29] Prime Minister Borden, sputtering with anger, rushed

[26] Canada, *H. of C. Debates,* 1916, II, Feb. 22, 1916, 992.
[27] Skilling, *op. cit.,* p. 57.
[28] Final Report of the Imperial Munitions Board to the Minister of Munitions, Flavelle Papers.
[29] Perley to Borden, March 4, 1916, Borden Papers, box 292.

to the defense. "There are no more loyal men in Canada than Directors and General Manager of that Company," he cabled back to London.[30] Out of collision came compromise. The Admiralty took two instead of four colliers.

The shipping problem, unlike the matter of orders for Canadian industry, never improved during the war. Aside from protest and an unsuccessful attempt to get representation on the Admiralty's requisitioning board, the only thing that could be done was to protect the few ships of Canadian registry. This was accomplished in a noteworthy Report of the Canadian Privy Council which denied the British right of requisition and declared: "It is the Parliament of Canada alone which constitutionally can determine and prescribe the burdens to be borne by this Dominion or by any of its citizens for the purposes of this or any other war."[31]

Sometimes by deliberate delay the Canadian government refused British demands. In April 1917 the Admiralty sought to requisition the *Empress of Russia* and the *Empress of Asia,* steamers trading between British Columbia and the Far East and owned by the Canadian Pacific Ocean Services, Ltd. The Canadian Pacific complained to the government,[32] and the government after six weeks of delay told the British that the ships were vital to Canada. "Trade in which they are employed at present time is not directly connected with conduct of war but is, on the other hand, a most important factor in development of Canadian resources, more especially those of the Province of British Columbia."[33] An impasse was reached. It lasted nearly a year. In January 1918 the Canadian government made the trade argument more explicit. The requisition of these ships "would practically mean the disappearance of British flag from Canadian Pacific ports, thus delivering this most important trade into Japanese hands. This trade once secured by Japanese, the process of wresting it from them after the war would be difficult if not impossible."[34] Finally the British brought the ultimate diplomatic pressure: a direct appeal from Lloyd George to Borden. Borden gave in.

[30] Borden to Perley, March 4, 1916, *ibid.*

[31] Quoted in Robert MacGregor Dawson, *The Development of Dominion Status, 1900-1936* (Toronto, 1937), p. 169.

[32] H. Maitland Kersey, managing director of the Canadian Pacific Ocean Services, Ltd., to Borden, April 30, 1917, Borden Papers, file OCA 89.

[33] Governor-General to Colonial Secretary (transmitting message from the Canadian Minister of Marine and Fisheries), June 14, 1917, Borden Papers, box 290.

[34] Governor-General to Colonial Secretary, Jan. 23, 1918, Borden Papers, file OCA 89.

3. The Problem of Military Control

Such issues were the day-to-day substance of wartime external affairs. To them must be added the special problem presented by Canada's military effort. When the first Canadian contingent arrived in England in October 1914 its status was uncertain; were these British Imperial troops no different from a division from Scotland or Wales or were they Canadians serving alongside the British but under control of the Canadian government? In 1914 the Canadian government had been quite happy to consider the troops Imperial in status, and completely under British control. But in the course of the war the second alternative, that of Canadian troops under Canadian control, was embraced by Canada and reluctantly accepted by the British. How this was done is a story of effective but irregular diplomacy.[35]

In September 1914 a British officer, Sir Edwin Alderson, was picked by Lord Kitchener to command the Canadian troops. The Canadian government had joined in the decision after concluding that no Canadian officer had sufficient experience for the job.[36] Relations between Alderson and the Canadian troops and government could not have been worse. Alderson considered the Canadians a colonial rabble requiring iron-handed discipline. As for the Canadian officers, he considered most of them too inexperienced to retain command. He and the War Office replaced many of them with British regulars. The Canadians in turn charged that Alderson and his staff cared more for the welfare of their dogs and polo ponies than for the men. Such a barrage of thoroughly unpleasant recriminations filled the air that a Canadian M. P. and future Prime Minister was moved to inquire after a trip abroad: "Are we fighting the English or the Germans?"[37]

Reports from the battle lines added to the bitterness. The sickening toll of casualties, the confusion and endless blunders—nearly inevitable results of trench warfare as it was then conducted—were

---

[35] Donald M. A. R. Vince has described some aspects of this process in two articles: "The Acting Overseas Sub-Militia Council and the Resignation of Sir Sam Hughes," *Canadian Historical Review*, XXXI (March 1950), 1-24; and "Development in the Legal Status of the Canadian Military Forces, 1914-1919, as related to Dominion Status," *Canadian Journal of Economics and Political Science*, XX (Aug. 1954), 357-370.

[36] Diary of Sir George Foster, Sept. 25, 1914.

[37] Richard B. Bennett to Borden, Dec. 7, 1915, Perley Papers, box 5.

blamed on British generals and Alderson in particular. In Canada the feeling seemed to be "growing very strongly everywhere that the British generals one and all are the most incompetent lot of bloody fools that have ever been collected together for the purpose of sacrificing armies in historic times."[38] So reported a Canadian living in British Columbia to his brother in England.

Whether such criticism was justified, the Canadian government could not allow matters to drag on unchanged. One expedient after another was tried in an effort to gain a degree of control over the Canadian troops. Sir Sam Hughes, the Minister of Militia, bellowed and blustered, had temper tantrums and burst into tears, ranted that British generals were "murderers," and predicted another "Boston tea party." He made enemies everywhere. Ultimately Borden dismissed him. Sir George Perley calmly took up problems one by one with the War Office, but Perley was apt to accept uncritically the British explanation for each difficulty. In addition an effective and unique arrangement was worked out with Sir Max Aitken (in 1917 Lord Beaverbrook), the Canadian-born *enfant terrible* of British politics.

Aitken gave the impression of doing everything at once. Press lord, member of parliament, active behind-the-scenes political manager, he took on multiple duties for the Canadian government. Early in the war he became official Canadian "eye witness" at the front, a sort of glorified newspaper reporter. Next he organized the Canadian War Records Office, a combination historical records section and propaganda agency. At the same time he acted as a diplomatic representative of the Canadian government, sending Borden and Hughes confidential reports, intervening in matters of promotion and appointment and even of military operations, and in April 1916 playing the key role in having General Alderson relieved of command.[39] Aitken, whose methods were colorful and direct, was an excellent troubleshooter, plunging into the midst of every difficulty after it appeared. But he was in no position to exercise any form of continuous supervision or to prevent problems from arising. For that purpose a fundamental reform and not a troubleshooter was needed.

[38] W. E. Oliver in Canada to his brother, F. S. Oliver in England, Nov. 24, 1915 in Stephen Gwynn, ed., *The Anvil of War* (London, 1936), p. 124.
[39] Aitken to Borden, April 26, 1916, Borden Papers, file OC 282.

The reform was carried through in the autumn of 1916 with the establishment of a Ministry of Overseas Forces from Canada with headquarters in London and with Perley, who continued to act as High Commissioner, as the first Minister. Perley was subsequently replaced by Sir Edward Kemp. A second landmark was the appointment in June 1917 of a Canadian, General Sir Arthur Currie, as commander of the Canadian Corps. Military problems continued to crop up after the establishment of the Overseas Ministry and the appointment of a Canadian as commander, but now there was a systematic way of dealing with those problems. The feeling of frustration and helplessness, so common in 1915, had disappeared.

4. The Search for New Procedures

Accompanying the Canadian government's efforts to build industry, protect shipping facilities, and gain control of the nation's military forces was an unending campaign to sweep away anachronistic forms which impeded the smooth operation of external affairs and to create new procedures and institutions which circumstances required.

In Canada there was the possibility of transforming the Department of External Affairs into a real, if miniature, foreign office where information was gathered and studied and where careful recommendations were drawn up. This was not done, and the reason was the character of the Under Secretary, Sir Joseph Pope. Sir Joseph was disturbed by the merest hint of innovation and lived looking backward to the days of Sir John A. Macdonald. If the department was to change, Sir Joseph would have to go, and Sir Joseph was useful as a file clerk and occasional runner of unimportant errands to Washington. Therefore, there would be no change. During the war the department was a backwater.

One individual nominally a member of the Department of External Affairs was, however, indispensable. That was the youthful Loring C. Christie, by title the Legal Advisor, in practice the Prime Minister's *fidus Achates*, idea man, confidential envoy and general right hand for external affairs. It was Christie who analyzed the messages from abroad, who drew up the key memoranda and drafted the cables that often set the tone and pattern of Canadian policy. When Borden went abroad, or to Washington, Christie was always at his elbow. Except for the Prime Minister no one played a larger part in external affairs. Christie by himself was Borden's foreign office. It is difficult to give him too much credit.

A nuisance in time of war was the creaking machinery for communicating with the British government through the medium of the Governor-General and the Secretary of State for the Colonies. This was particularly so because of the individuals who occupied those positions during the war. The Duke of Connaught, Queen Victoria's son, presented special difficulties as Governor-General. Naïvely he believed himself the real ruler of Canada and the literal commander-in-chief of the armed forces. Accordingly he attempted to interfere in matters large and small. In 1916 he was virtually driven back to England because of friction with the Canadian government. The crisis over Connaught was one more of inconvenience than of the constitution.[40] One practical result was that the Canadian government came increasingly to by-pass the Governor-General's office as a channel of communication. Another result was that Borden concluded it would be wise to have a Canadian as Governor-General in the future.[41]

The fact that normal channels passed through the Colonial Office was also an annoyance, in large measure because the post of Colonial Secretary was never well filled during the war. Lewis Harcourt, who held the office until May 1915, was not a man of energy or imagination. Bonar Law, who followed, was fully occupied with his leadership of the Conservative party and neglected the Colonial Office job. Walter Long, who took over when the Lloyd George Government was formed in December 1916, was a slight improvement. Long tried valiantly to please but was painfully conservative. In character and outlook he suggests an English version of Sir Joseph Pope. As the war progressed the Colonial Secretary was increasingly ignored by the Canadian government. Instead the High Commissioner in London was used whenever possible as, in effect, an ambassador to Great Britain. Perley, in spite of his own conservative tendencies, rapidly came to assume heavy responsibilities.

[40] Borden reported on his difficulties with the Duke in the *Memoirs*, II, 601-604; far more is revealed in the Borden Papers.

[41] Writing after the war to Bonar Law, Borden stated that in 1916 he had toyed with the idea of having Sir Wilfrid Laurier succeed the Duke of Connaught as Governor-General. Borden to Bonar Law, Jan. 10, 1923, Borden Papers, post-1921 correspondence, folder 148. Certainly this would have been an ingenious way of kicking a tough political opponent upstairs.

For the first two and a half years of the war Canadian external affairs were conducted in a halting, uncertain fashion. Beyond the natural concentration on immediate material interests (which at all times remained fundamental) there was little search for larger goals, little attempt to look beyond the end of the war or to ponder the nature of Canada's future international relations. The explanation for this provincial lack of vision and even lack of dignity is easily found. First, the British government for more than two years, despite pious words to the contrary, did not regard Canada as a responsible separate nation whose views should be sought and listened to. Secondly, it is not to be expected that the Canadian government would overnight acquire the outlook and the confidence to think independently on international issues. Thirdly, the war during this period was a singularly discouraging affair, seemingly endless. And with no end of the war in sight it was futile to look beyond the needs of the immediate day. A significant change took place, however, in the year 1917. The change was the result of three developments: the creation of the Imperial War Cabinet, the entry of the United States into the war, and the formation of the Union Government, a coalition of Conservatives and English-speaking Liberals, in Canada.

David Lloyd George became Prime Minister of Great Britain in December 1916 and immediately made plans for the calling together of the so-called Imperial War Cabinet, which met for the first time in March 1917. It is easily the best known development in the wartime relations of Great Britain and the Dominions. A good deal of nonsense was written at the time about the supposedly transcendent implications of this institution. Ardent "new Imperialists" rejoiced that here was a device that would save the Empire and create a great and lasting unity. Professional defenders of Dominion autonomy smelled a plot. In practice the Imperial War Cabinet was neither plot nor panacea. It was simply a well-organized consultation of Prime Ministers and heads of departments, men with views to exchange and policies to co-ordinate if possible. Through the discussions of the Imperial War Cabinet the Canadian government for the first time acquired the information with which to build an over-all view of the war in order to plan more than twenty-four hours ahead. For the first time, also, there was the opportunity to examine the objectives of the war with knowledgeable care and to debate the tangled question of peace terms.

Meeting on alternate days during the same weeks as the Imperial War Cabinets of 1917 and 1918 were a pair of Imperial War Conferences presided over by the Colonial Secretary but given little close attention by the heads of government. The Conferences were sideshows of windy debate on matters of less immediate importance. Their main accomplishment was to churn forth a set of resolutions and proceedings to put before the public. It was in the Imperial Conferences that enthusiastic economic centralizers, like W. A. S. Hewins, then Under Secretary of the Colonial Office, had their day creating a paper model for a closed and economically integrated postwar British Empire.[42] The response of the Canadian government to this activity was skeptical and standoffish.

5. The United States: From Neutral Neighbor to Cobelligerent

The entry of the United States into the war in April 1917 was of even greater importance than the creation of the Imperial War Cabinet. The end of American neutrality meant the end not only of petty irritations but the release of a serious subconscious tension in Canadian external affairs, a tension resulting from the inability to ground war policy on an understanding with the United States as well as on direct Canadian and Imperial interests. Now that opportunity had arrived.

Prime Minister Borden had never taken easily to that tweaking of Uncle Sam's whiskers that was stock in trade for many politicians in the Canadian Conservative party. Understanding American problems, he never showed resentment at United States neutrality. Under Borden's direction Canadian policy towards the United States from 1914 until the American declaration of war was characterized by economic competition but extreme political circumspection. When American boys ran away to enlist in Canada and their worried parents wanted them home, Canadian authorities bent over backwards to oblige. When the Canadian public was on edge over the imagined threat of an attack on Canada by Germans living in the United States, the government threw cold water on the alarms.

[42] W. K. Hancock, *Survey of British Commonwealth Affairs* (London, 1937, 1940, 1942) has a section on the "Economics of Siege" in Part I of Volume II, *Problems of Economic Policy*, pp. 94-110, which admirably captures the outlook of this group. See also W. A. S. Hewins, *The Apologia of an Imperialist* 2 vols. (London, 1929).

One episode involving a sharp Anglo-American controversy well illustrates the circumspect Canadian attitude. In September 1916 relations between the United States and Great Britain were badly strained owing to the coincidence of galling British use of the "black list" against American firms and the tensions of the American presidential campaign. President Wilson, in order to strengthen his protests against the British "black list" practice, had secured the passage through Congress of legislation giving him the power to place an embargo on the export of all munitions. British Ambassador to Washington Sir Cecil Spring-Rice was thrown into a panic. If the embargo were imposed, and he feared it would be, the British war effort might be fatally handicapped. Spring-Rice's own protests to the American government seemed to be unheeded. What could be done? Spring-Rice thought of Canada and dashed off a quick note to Borden describing the crisis as "so serious that it is impossible to foresee the consequences" and suggesting that "it might be useful, considering the very friendly feeling here towards Canada, if a private warning came from your Government. . . . It had better not come through me as it would only be duplicating language already held."[43] Three days later the Colonial Secretary, Bonar Law, cabled the same advice but used more emphatic language:

We believe it essential to represent to the Government of the United States the grave effect of any retaliatory measures. . . . If, as we believe, cordial relations with the Dominion of Canada are one of the chief concerns of the United States Government, we believe that an intimation to the President of the lamentable effect of such measures on Canadian opinion might have great influence.[44]

That was strong urging, but to Borden the idea of such Canadian intervention in this instance was repugnant. After consulting his colleagues Borden decided against action. In the first place he considered that Wilson was only bluffing and would never impose the embargo; thus a Canadian protest would accomplish nothing except to run the risk of irritating the United States.[45] The protest would also give the impression, which Borden wanted to avoid, that Canada was acting the diplomatic puppet of Great Britain. The episode passed. Borden was right in thinking the embargo would never be

[43] Spring-Rice to Borden, Sept. 17, 1916, Borden Papers, file OC 306.
[44] Colonial Secretary to the Governor-General, Sept. 20, 1916, *ibid.*
[45] Borden to Perley, Sept. 20, 1916, Perley Papers, box 6.

imposed, and the Canadian government had the satisfaction of knowing it had not risked its reputation in Washington. Canadian policy in this instance may have been negative, but it was independent.

Once the United States was in the war the Canadian government considered that the time for reticence was over. Now was the time to begin working for a distinct Canadian-American understanding, something akin to but apart from the relations between the United States and Great Britain. In press and Parliament there were innumerable idealistic rejoicings over the new partnership between Canada and the United States. A typical panegyric was that of W. F. Maclean in the House of Commons:

We find ourselves today a great democratic community on the American continent, joined up with the United States in asserting the rights of civilization as against autocracy. . . . We must realize that to-day America, . . . the centre of the world and the centre of democracy, with that outlook, and with its resources controls the situation, and if it believes—as it does believe—in democracy, then we shall win.[46]

In more practical terms the Canadian government faced the problem of how to open up direct ties with the United States, the avenues of communication necessary for a truly effective, as opposed to an orator's, partnership. The obvious answer was the establishment of separate Canadian diplomatic representation in Washington. The project was actively discussed from the moment the United States declared war, but, because of the demands of the political crisis over conscription in Canada, it was not until October 1917 that details were worked out. By then the first envoy, J. D. Hazen, formerly Minister of the Naval Service, had been picked by Borden and was ready to depart for Washington. But at the last minute a coalition of conservative-minded Canadians and Englishmen—Sir George Foster, Sir Cecil Spring-Rice, and Walter Long, with a probable assist from Sir Joseph Pope—combined to delay the move. Borden was miffed and in February 1918 settled for the establishment of a Canadian War Mission instead. This mission, headed by the businessman Lloyd Harris, worked to co-ordinate economic policies but never performed any political function.[47]

[46] Canada, *H. of C. Debates*, 1918, II, May 14, 1951-1952, 1953.
[47] G. P. deT. Glazebrook, *A History of Canadian External Relations* (Toronto, 1950), pp. 365-367, presents a summary view of the unsuccessful wartime attempt to establish direct representation in Washington. The full, complicated story can be followed in the Borden Papers.

All this was frustrating and it was made doubly so by the old story of American government ignorance of and indifference to Canada. Canada was too close to be noticed. The State Department paid no attention to the Dominion. The reports of U. S. consuls in Canada were seldom very perceptive and were almost never read in Washington by anyone of authority. President Wilson—unlike his predecessors Theodore Roosevelt and William Howard Taft— was totally uninformed about Canada and seemed to regard it, at least until 1918, as a non-self-governing territory. Colonel Edward M. House, who might have been expected to enlighten Wilson, rather surprisingly had only a dim notion of Canada and never met a member of the Canadian government before 1919. Secretary of State Robert Lansing had friends in Canada but resisted to the point of rudeness repeated attempts by the Canadian government in 1917 and 1918 to have him visit Ottawa.[48]

Lack of diplomatic contact and, on the American side, equal lack of understanding would seem to indicate that political relations between Canada and the United States during the war must have been non-existent. This, however, was not the case as the culminating period of Canadian wartime external affairs—June to December 1918—demonstrates.

6. The Climax of Wartime Diplomacy

The formation of the Union Government in October 1917 and the victory of that government over the Sir Wilfrid Laurier rump of the Liberal party in the animus-filled elections of December 1917 pulled Canada out of the worst period of its great internal wartime crisis. Gone from the Cabinet were several mediocre Conservative politicians who had been a discrediting burden to their colleagues and a constant source of worry to Prime Minister Borden. In their places were a group of able English-speaking Liberals, men who had broken with Laurier over the conscription issue. After the election of 1917 Borden ceased to toy despondently with the idea of resignation, as he had done almost continuously until then. No longer was the government inhibited by the uncertain fear of possible defeat.

[48] The sources for this paragraph are the files of the Department of State in the National Archives, Washington; the papers of Woodrow Wilson and Robert Lansing in the Library of Congress; the papers of Edward M. House and Frank L. Polk in the Yale University Library, New Haven, Connecticut.

This is not the place to enter into a discussion of the great "Crisis of Quebec" which disfigured Canadian political life during the war. But it is worth noting that the Cabinet of 1917 contained only two French Canadians, and they were men without influence. This was symptomatic of the political estrangement of the races that grew so complete during the war that it was inconceivable to the English-speaking Canadians who monopolized the government that French Canada might have any views on external policy worth heeding in the slightest degree. During World War I Canadian government was not a process of compromise; it was an English-speaking government with the French minority half driven, half hiding in political exile.

With political reorganization at home preparing the way for the more confident conduct of external policy, the Prime Minister found himself surrounded now by new men whose abilities could be put to good use. For external affairs the most impressive figure in the Union Government, after Borden, was the Liberal Newton W. Rowell, a man whose interest in Canada's international position was fully as great as Borden's. The outlook of the two men was similar, although Rowell was more apt to talk in terms of ideals and morality. With Rowell and Borden acting together, Canadian external policy became concerned as never before with broad world considerations. This is not to say that the persistent themes of economic interest were abandoned. Instead many of the day-to-day details of shipping, orders, markets, and the like were put in the hands of a covey of special boards and missions. Borden cared just as much as ever that those details were watched over in Canada's interest, but now it was only on infrequent occasions that he personally had to do the watching.

The expanded nature of external affairs in 1918 was evident in many areas. One episode may be taken as an illustration: Canada's participation in the Siberian intervention.[49] This single affair entailed a blending of many strands of external policy: the desire to take a greater part in military strategy as well as to have direct control of Canadian troops, the drive to expand Canadian overseas markets, and the wish to keep generally in step with the United States. Also, of course, it required Canada to wrestle briefly with the problem of Bolshevik Russia.

[49] Discussed at greater length in the author's "Canada and the Siberian Intervention, 1918-1919" *American Historical Review*, LXIV (July, 1959), 866-877.

When Borden, Rowell, and other members of the Cabinet arrived in London in June 1918 for the second series of meetings of the Imperial War Cabinet, the military prospects on the Western front were bleak. The Allies were still in a state of shock from the German spring offensive; the direct military weight of the United States had not yet been applied. To the Canadian government it appeared that the incompetence of British generals might lead to complete defeat in Europe. For a year a Canadian had been in command of the Canadian Corps, but now it was time to speak out and attempt to influence the military strategy to which the Canadian divisions were bound. Accordingly on June 13 at the Imperial War Cabinet Borden delivered an impassioned indictment of the conduct of the war.[50]

Lloyd George, delighted to find Borden such a vocal ally in his own feud with the generals, moved quickly to set up a special committee of Prime Ministers for the purpose of plotting out grand strategy for the rest of the war. In its report the committee recommended that major offensive operations on the Western front be postponed until 1919, preferably until 1920. As one alternative to following in the same old rut in the West the attempt to draw Russia back into the war and re-create an Eastern front was to be pressed.[51] This ambitious scheme had been under continuous discussion since late 1917. Its success depended, so it was believed, on Japanese and American participation. But President Wilson was adamant in opposition. He feared the effects of Japan's presence in Siberia. The Japanese, for their part, did not want to antagonize the United States. By June 1918 there was complete deadlock and no intervention. At this point the British War Office decided that the British ought to go it alone. The great problem was lack of troops. Perhaps Canada could oblige and send five thousand directly across the Pacific to Vladivostok. Borden, agreeing with the basic military premise that intervention might succeed in opening an Eastern front, approved the request. But by the time the details could be worked out, the situation had changed. The war was nearly over in Europe, and the United States, having veered suddenly about and become an intervening power, seemed to have a policy that conflicted with British, and thus Canadian, aims.

[50] Borden, *Memoirs*, II, 808-814.
[51] Report of the Committee of Prime Ministers on War Policy, Borden Papers, file OC 628.

In August the majority of the Canadian Cabinet felt the expedition should be called off. But not the Prime Minister. Borden now came forward with a direct appeal to Canadian economic interests:

Intimate relations with that rapidly developing country [Siberia] will be of great advantage to Canada in the future. Other nations will make very vigorous and determined efforts to obtain a foothold and our interposition with a small military force would tend to bring Canada into favourable notice by the strongest elements in that great community.[52]

Borden's view prevailed. After the Canadian government had assured itself that the expedition was completely under Ottawa's control, the troops went forward. They arrived in Vladivostok just as the war in Europe was coming to an end thus ending the original anti-German argument for intervention. Sharp conflicts in policy appeared among the different intervening powers, and the Canadians found themselves aligned in attitude with the Americans against the Japanese and the British—an uncomfortable position. As for the economic interest, it was sharply denied now that the war was over. "Canada has no such economic or business interests as will justify the employment of a Canadian force composed of young men whose parents and friends desire should return at once to their ordinary occupations," was the conclusion of the Cabinet in Ottawa.[53]

Gradually the Prime Minister reconsidered his position, and on December 30 made a pair of important related announcements to the Imperial War Cabinet. First, he said, a British policy that meant working in co-operation with another power against the United States could not count on the support of Canada. Second, it was senseless to continue intervention in Russia. The only thing to do was have a conference with all Russian factions, including the Bolsheviks.[54] Those statements marked the fact that Borden was ready to call the Canadian expedition back from Siberia. The British War Office wanted the Canadians to stay. Borden said no. Shortly thereafter the withdrawal began. For the first time the Canadian government had acted independently in a major matter of world policy outside the "North Atlantic triangle." The diplomatic unity of the British

[52] Borden to S. C. Mewburn (Minister of Militia and Defence), Aug. 13, 1918, Borden Papers, file OC 518.
[53] Sir Thomas White (Acting Prime Minister in Ottawa) to Borden (in London), Nov. 25, 1918, *ibid.*
[54] Minutes of the Imperial War Cabinet, Dec. 30, 1918, Borden Papers, box 333.

Empire was fine enough in theory, but in this instance it was deemed unwise to march in step with the British.

Although the Siberian intervention has been described in some detail, other episodes could be used to illustrate the nature of Canadian external affairs in the closing months of the war. The Siberian episode, however, is the best illustration of the growth of Canada's policies in external affairs during the war. Between 1914 and 1918 there were many differences, but the principal one was that by the latter year the Canadian government had acquired an awareness of Canada as an international entity capable of pursuing responsible policies. No longer was Canada simply a passive adjunct of Great Britain in world affairs outside the direct purview of the Atlantic triangle; no longer was the duty of the Canadian government in its conduct of external affairs conceived of as being limited to the advancement of immediate interests on the North American continent.

Pragmatically and without ever consciously pausing to think in terms of unified policy, the Canadian government had gradually formed a rough outline of objectives for external policy. The key to them all can be seen in an entry Sir Robert Borden made in his diary while in London, December 1, 1918. It was late at night, but before going to bed he dutifully recorded the activities of the day. The morning, he noted, had been spent pondering over documents from the British Foreign Office and the War Cabinet. The outlook was discouraging. Throughout Europe Bolshevism was reported on the march. In the afternoon he had watched the triumphal arrival in London of Marshal Foch, but now as he wrote the Canadian Prime Minister could not keep his mind on pageantry. His thoughts ranged restlessly between past and future. Back to August, 1914. Ahead to the uncertain future. Borden pondered, and then continued writing: "I am beginning to feel that in the end and perhaps sooner than later, Canada must assume full sovereignty. She can give better service to G[reat] B[ritain] & [the] U[nited] S[tates] & to the world in that way."[55]

Full sovereignty, recognition of Canada's separate international status, was thus the foundation stone of external policy at war's end. This was not simply a matter of hollow prestige. Borden was then well on his way to achieving that objective for Canada through his

[55] Diary of Sir Robert Borden, Dec. 1, 1918. In possession of Henry Borden, Esquire, Toronto, Ontario. Used by kind permission.

successful insistence that the Dominions have separate representation at the Paris Peace Conference and subsequently full membership in the League of Nations. As a corollary to full sovereignty Borden hoped to see the immediate establishment of direct Canadian diplomatic relations with the United States, the project which had been thwarted during the war. On this point a combination of circumstances brought about the continued defeat of Borden's wish. A Canadian legation in Washington was not opened until 1927.

The second major foundation stone of external policy in 1918 was strenuous advocacy of full co-operation between the United States and Great Britain on all essential issues, with Canada to have the right to be disassociated from British policy if that co-operation were ever placed in jeopardy. To implement this objective Borden and his colleagues (here Rowell played a leading part) opposed a peace settlement that would bring territorial gains to Great Britain while advocating that the United States assume responsibility for the guidance of "backward" peoples, in former German East Africa, for example.[56] In addition the Canadian government was fully in favor of the creation of some sort of league of nations. On other matters in which the occasion arose to express an opinion, Canada stood for rigorous but not crippling peace terms for Germany. Borden considered heavy demands for reparations unreasonable if not impossible.[57] Belatedly and influenced by members of his Cabinet Borden also came to favor immediate liquidation of intervention in Russia.

This was hardly a comprehensive program, but it represented, with all its gaps and weaknesses, tremendous growth in external policy since 1914. Thus the stage was set for the Paris Peace Conference[58] and the short span of illusioned interwar years. The degree to which these Canadian aims of 1918 were to be fulfilled, forgotten, or engulfed belongs to the history of that period.

[56] Borden, had he known, might well have been discouraged by President Woodrow Wilson's reaction to the Canadian position. "England will want the German colonies," said Wilson on board the George Washington on his way to the Peace Conference. "Mr. [sic] Borden, the Canadian premier, has declared that Canada would be opposed to the mother country's acquiring any more colonies. He incidentally expressed the desire that the German colonies be turned over to the United States, if to anybody. Of course, we don't want them and wouldn't have them. . . ." Quoted by Arthur Walworth, Woodrow Wilson (New York, 1958), II, 217.

[57] David Lloyd George, Memoirs of the Peace Conference (New Haven, 1939), I, 318, quoting minutes of a meeting of the Imperial War Cabinet in December, 1918.

[58] See G. P. deT. Glazebrook, Canada at the Paris Peace Conference (Toronto, 1942).

4

"A Low Dishonest Decade": Aspects of Canadian External Policy, 1931-1939

James Eayrs

There has not yet taken place in Canada that debate on the wisdom of appeasement in which British statesmen and scholars have been engaged since the appearance of Professor Feiling's *Life of Neville Chamberlain.* If this seems a remarkable fact, it is not hard to explain. Had the Canadian government of that day urged a more sturdy resistance to the Nazi tyranny, it is doubtful that events would have taken a significantly different course. German policy was unresponsive to the action or inaction of the Dominions; and it seems unlikely that Chamberlain would have been deflected from the path of the appeaser any more by the Prime Minister of Canada than he was by the Prime Minister of New Zealand, which is to say not at all. Canada's external policy during the years 1931-1939, so far from requiring extended apology, appears to most of its historians to possess the self-evident vindication of having brought a united and determined nation to Britain's side on September 10, 1939. The evidence which might sustain a contrary interpretation is still scanty. Documents from the files of the Department of External Affairs have yet to be published; the private papers of the Prime Ministers of the period are withheld from the scholar's domain;[1] both R. B. Bennett and Mackenzie King retained a jealous hold upon the External Affairs portfolio and conducted foreign policy possessively,

---

[1] The Bennett Papers have been deposited by Lord Beaverbrook, their owner, at the Library of the University of New Brunswick. The King Papers are in the Public Archives of Canada and become the property of the Crown in 1975. The present writer, having assisted in the preparation of the official biography of W. L. Mackenzie King, has had access to this immense collection; he has permission from Mr. King's Literary Executors to quote from the King correspondence to the end of 1923, the period covered by the published first volume of the official biography.

even stealthily, so that few of their colleagues and subordinates have been able to throw strong light upon shadowy though crucial episodes; and a tradition unlike that prevailing at Westminster (where politics and literature—or politics and journalism—honorably combine) assists in their concealment. These are some (but by no means all) of the circumstances accounting for the remarkable early appearance of an Authorized Version of events not yet three decades removed.

The time is now approaching when a revisionist interpretation will be possible; one or two significant steps in this direction have already been taken.[2] The present paper has a more modest purpose. It attempts to discuss some aspects of Canadian external policy during the 1930's to which insufficient attention has perhaps been paid, and to bring to more familiar themes evidence previously overlooked. Although the title[3] may suggest an excess of moral indignation, its point of view is rather that of Lord Vansittart, who, writing of Dominion policies during the period in which he labored with such prescience and to such little avail, remarked, perhaps too generously: "One could not blame them, one could not admire them, one could not admire anybody."[4]

1. The New World and the Old

In 1919 Canadians turned away from Europe, leaving behind their dead. However misguided it might appear to those of a later generation drawn as their fathers had been into "the vortex of militarism," isolationism in Canada was a natural response to the four-year ordeal on the Western front. The Great War remade the map, but left unchanged the scale and the projection. How could a conflict in which major gains were measured by hundreds of yards, and a million lives exchanged for a few desolated acres of mud, affect in any way the traditional concepts of geography? It brought half a million Canadians to Europe but Europe no closer to Canada. The world was still wide. To the Oceans and the Fleet might now be

---

[2] See K. W. McNaught, "Canadian Foreign Policy and the Whig Interpretation: 1936-1939," Canadian Historical Association, *Report of the Annual Meeting* 1957, pp. 43-54.

[3] It is taken from the poem by W. H. Auden, "September 1, 1939": "As the clever hopes expire/Of a low dishonest decade."

[4] *The Mist Procession: The Autobiography of Lord Vansittart* (London, 1958), p. 529.

added as purveyor of security the great and friendly guardian to the South. Canada was "a fire-proof house, far from inflammable materials";[5] and its fortunate inhabitants peered indistinctly at the distant continent from which invasion seemed so improbable. "At present danger of attack upon Canada is minor in degree and second-hand in origin," Mackenzie King had insisted as late as 1938;[6] and although his military advisers were less certain of Canada's immunity,[7] their misgivings were not allowed to disturb unduly the complacency of the public or the size of the defense estimates.

Isolationism was the product of geography; it was shaped by distrust, a distrust born of the Great War and confirmed at the council tables of Paris. "It was European policy, European statesmanship, European ambition, that drenched this world with blood," N. W. Rowell told the First Assembly of the League of Nations. "Fifty thousand Canadians under the soil of France and Flanders is what Canada has paid for European statesmanship trying to settle European problems. I place responsibility on a few; I would not distribute it over many; but nevertheless it is European."[8] These bluntly accusing words, an official of the Canadian delegation wrote privately at the time, "hurt and stung many people," and in his view "marred the performance."[9] But they conveyed, however tactlessly, the sense of Canadian feeling; and the Prime Minister wrote to their author to express his "appreciation of the stand you took in stating to the Conference, as frankly as you did, the price the world has paid for the European diplomacy of the last hundred years."[10] Nor, as it seemed, had the trauma of the trenches changed Europe for the better. Ancient enmities and grievances arose once more, or were replaced or supplemented by new disorders; the scope for intrigue and for disaster was if anything enhanced. "Everywhere there are signs of trouble," wrote one of Canada's representatives at the Paris Peace Conference in 1919. "Egypt is now disturbed with the fever

[5] League of Nations, Official Journal, Special Supplement No. 23, Records of the Fifth Assembly (1924), p. 222. It is interesting that this most celebrated of Canadian utterances on foreign affairs goes unremarked in the unpublished autobiography of Senator Raoul Dandurand, its author.
[6] Canada, House of Commons Debates, 1938, III, 3179.
[7] See Colonel C. P. Stacey, Six Years of War: The Army in Canada, Britain and the Pacific (Ottawa, 1955), p. 10.
[8] League of Nations, Records of the First Assembly (1920), p. 379.
[9] Loring C. Christie to Sir Robert Borden, Dec. 12, 1920, Borden Papers (Public Archives of Canada).
[10] Arthur Meighen to N. W. Rowell, Jan. 10, 1921, Rowell Papers (P.A.C.).

for self govt.—the vicious results of Wilson's doctrine of ill or non-defined self determination. Asia Minor and Turkey are disorganized —Roumanians threatened on three sides by Bolshevists and Hungarians—Russia poisoned and poisoning—Hungary communist and Germany in near chaos. 'Tis surely a sad mess out of which to evolve a new Europe."[11]

Distrust and disapproval of Europe's statecraft and statesmen passed easily into an assertion of North American moral superiority. In Canada as in the United States there was nourished the conviction that the New World in its national life and international behavior exhibited standards above and beyond those of the Old. Like Mr. Herbert Hoover, Canadians

returned in 1919 from several years abroad . . . steeped with two ideas: first, that through three hundred years [North] America had developed something new in a way of life of a people, which transcended all others of history; and second, that out of the boiling social and economic cauldron of Europe, with its hates and fears, rose miasmic infections which might greatly harm or even destroy . . . the hope of the world.[12]

Rare was the Canadian who, addressing himself at Geneva or at home to the theme of his country's place in world affairs, did not elaborate this contrast. ". . . we think in terms of peace," remarked Senator Dandurand in 1924, "while Europe, an armed camp, thinks in terms of war."[13] "After listening to and participating in the proceedings of the League," Mackenzie King declared in 1928, "I have come back to Canada with a more profound conviction than ever that there is no land on the face of the globe in which the lot of men, women and children is cast in a pleasanter place than in this Dominion."[14] In 1936 he referred to Canada's "tremendous, absorbing and paramount tasks of achieving economic development and national unity, which with us take the place of the preoccupation with the fear of attack and the dreams of glory which beset older and more crowded countries";[15] a few weeks later, at Geneva, he contrasted his coun-

[11] Diary of Sir George Foster, entry for April 7, 1919 (P.A.C.).

[12] *The Memoirs of Herbert Hoover: The Cabinet and the Presidency, 1920-1933* (New York, 1951), p. v.

[13] League of Nations, Official Journal, Special Supplement No. 23, *Records of the Fifth Assembly* (1924), p. 221.

[14] "Address Delivered by the Right Hon. W. L. Mackenzie King on November 9th, 1928, at a Banquet of the League of Nations Society in Canada" (Ottawa, 1928), p. 22.

[15] Canada, *H. of C. Debates*, 1936, IV, 3862.

try's friendly relations with the United States and Europe's "violent . . . propaganda and recriminations hurled incessantly across the frontiers, the endeavours [in Europe] to draw all countries into one or other extremist camp, the feverish race for rearmament, the hurrying to and fro of diplomats, the ceaseless weaving and unravelling of understandings and alliances, and the consequent fear and uncertainty of the peoples";[16] and in March 1939, soon after Hitler's seizure of Czechoslovakia, he referred despairingly to the "continent that cannot run itself," in implied contrast to that North American continent which could.[17]

Such comparisons were frequently joined to moral exhortation. The rostrum of the Palais des Nations became for successive Canadian spokesmen a pulpit from which Europe was urged to forswear her foolish ways, to abandon intrigue, violence, hostility, to adopt those institutions which (they claimed) had brought a century of peace to North America. Canada and the United States, Mackenzie King informed the Ninth Assembly of the League of Nations, had ceased "to rely upon force, we have looked to reason as the method of solving our differences, and reason has supplied us from time to time with conference, conciliation or arbitration in a form . . . sufficient to settle our various differences as they have arisen."[18] Let there be a European Rush-Bagot Treaty, a European International Joint Commission—tranquillity would follow for a hundred years. As a prescription for Old World ills, these New World remedies were altogether inadequate, arising as they did from a wholly different situation.

> The toad beneath the harrow knows
> Exactly where each tooth-point goes;
> The butterfly upon the road
> Preaches contentment to that toad.

Moreover, they were compounded of a series of fictions unrelated to things as they were. "Not a single soldier, not a single cannon," the Canadian delegate had told the Fifth Assembly of the League, faced the famous frontier. This was simple falsehood. The International Joint Commission had been able to function without major difficulty

[16] League of Nations, *Verbatim Record of the Seventeenth Ordinary Session of the Assembly*, Sept. 29, 1936, p. 1.
[17] Canada, *H. of C. Debates*, 1939, III, 2419.
[18] League of Nations, Official Journal, Special Supplement No. 64, *Records of the Ninth Assembly* (1928), p. 60.

only because each government had refrained from submitting disputes other than those over waterways. As for the Rush-Bagot Agreement, "the truth is," Mackenzie King had written privately in 1922, "our American friends have been steadily evading [it], until it has become more or less of a mockery to speak of its terms in the manner in which we do."[19]

However ill-justified, Canada's moralizing at Europe led logically not to isolation but engagement. Ought not the practitioners of the New World's higher morality try by more active participation in the affairs of the Old to lead it into the paths of righteousness? That is not what happened. More potent than the zeal of the missionary was the desire to escape contamination. The less the New World came in contact with the Old, the better; the more, the greater the chance of succumbing to those "miasmic infections" which threatened to invade and to destroy the healthy bodies politic of North America. "Bolshevism," wrote the editor of the *Canadian Annual Review* in 1918, "had a basis wherever Russians and Jews and other foreigners gathered together" in Canada's cities; if foreigners brought Bolshevism, Canadians should keep clear of foreigners. "We are told there are enormous numbers of people on the continent of Europe who want to come [here]," remarked a former Minister of Immigration in 1922. "I want to say I regard it of the dimensions of a national menace that there is any danger whatever of the bars being let down."[20] Questioned in 1920 on Canada's readiness to accept a mandate for Armenia, the Leader of the Opposition wrote that the proposal "would provoke general protest from one end of the Dominion to the other," for "a sort of reaction has set in . . . with respect to interference by the Governments of this Continent with European Affairs."[21] As the twenty years' crisis developed and deepened, isolationism became if anything more firmly rooted in the Canadian people and their governors. Early in 1922 the Canadian government refused to contribute funds in the form of an interest-free loan for the relief of famine in Russia, and turned down a Soviet request for credit to buy Canadian seed wheat. In 1924 it ignored an appeal to contribute to the relief of famine in Albania.

[19] Mackenzie King to Wallace Nesbitt, Oct. 2, 1922, King Papers.
[20] Sir Clifford Sifton, "Immigration," in *Addresses Delivered before the Canadian Club of Toronto, 1921-2* (Toronto, 1923), pp. 185-186.
[21] Mackenzie King to Aneuran Williams, Feb. 18, 1920, King Papers. A portion of this letter is quoted in R. MacGregor Dawson, *William Lyon Mackenzie King: A Political Biography*, Vol. I, *1874-1923* (Toronto, 1958), p. 404.

In 1925 it refused the invitation to sign the Geneva Protocol, and it was largely at Canada's insistence that an article was inserted in the text of the Locarno Agreements specifically exempting the Dominions from their provisions. ". . . I do not see," Ernest Lapointe observed some years later, "that Canada should assume obligations in connection with the boundaries between France and Germany . . . [or] guarantee any boundaries in central Europe or elsewhere. . . ."[22] And an influential member of the Canadian government wrote before sailing for the Imperial Conference in the spring of 1937:

The conference will be interesting, and probably in some ways revealing; but the more I see of the whole thing, the more I am certain that our destiny is on the North American continent and that if Europe is going to insist on destroying itself, it is no part of our mission to destroy ourselves in attempting to prevent it. . . .[23]

2. *The League and the Nation*

If other countries entered the League of Nations in something of the spirit expressed by Smuts' phrase—"the tents have been struck and the great caravan of humanity is once more on the march"—Canada may be said to have been mainly concerned lest she be called upon to do more than her share of the work in breaking camp or be compelled to march without the consent of her Parliament. It is usual to attribute the reserve with which Canadians watched the Geneva experiment to the coercive characteristics of the Covenant, and to suppose that so long as the League confined itself to conciliatory methods it could count upon Canadian approval. This view has the weighty support of Professor Mansergh, who writes that "from the first the League was welcomed as a means of furthering international co-operation, as a forum for debate and discussion," and that it was only "as a means for enforcing, as distinct from maintaining, peace" that it aroused the suspicion and censure of successive Canadian governments.[24] Certainly it is difficult to overestimate the agitated concern lest through Articles X and XVI of the Covenant the newly independent Dominion be placed at "the beck and call of a Council not responsible to the nation for its actions," or, even worse,

[22] Canada, *H. of C. Debates*, 1928, II, 1960.
[23] T. A. Crerar to J. W. Dafoe, April 17, 1937, Dafoe Papers (P.A.C.)
[24] Nicholas Mansergh, *Survey of British Commonwealth Affairs: Problems of External Policy, 1931-1939* (London, 1952), p. 112.

become involved "in conflicts in some far-away section of Europe, or in some distant portion of South America."[25] Fears such as these lead to that policy, "remarkable," as Professor Mansergh observes, "for its consistency," by which Canada tried at first to have Article X removed entirely from the Covenant; that proving unsuccessful, introduced an interpretative resolution which, though it failed by one vote to receive the unanimous support required for adoption, had the desired effect of weakening the obligations of League membership; and finally, when the League was confronted with the two decisive tests of its procedures for collective security, did what could be done to weaken the effectiveness of sanctions.

But this interpretation may be misleading. It implies a degree of attachment to the League as a non-coercive agency for peaceful conciliation which, whatever might be said in public, no Canadian Minister really felt. For Canadian suspicion of Geneva derived basically from Canadian distrust of Europe; and it was as a European institution that the League appeared from Canada. "The League was born ostensibly as a world League," commented a former official of the Department of External Affairs in 1926, "but really is a European League with the non-Europeans tacked on. The most distinctive and powerful New World people went out of it." A Canadian had no more legitimate concern "with the administration of Danzig or of the Saar Valley" than had "a Nova Scotian . . . [with] the municipal government of Vancouver."[26] "Let us . . . conciliate Quebec and Ontario," remarked a member of Parliament in 1923, "before we start conciliating Roumania and Ukrainia."[27] "The League of Nations is a preposterous and expensive farce," wrote Sir Clifford Sifton, "and amounts to nothing more than a part of a machine designed to involve us in European and Imperialistic complications. Canada ought to call a halt on this business."[28] The views of those in office were much the same. Sir Joseph Pope, the Under Secretary of State for External Affairs until 1925, dismissed the Covenant as "not worth the paper it is written on," and wrote in his diary: "Our reps are making a great stir at the League of Nations, advertizing Canada and incidentally themselves. I think it all

[25] Canada, H. of C. Debates, 1919 (Special Session), pp. 102, 103.
[26] Loring C. Christie, "Notes on the League of Nations Meeting of March, 1926," April 14, 1926, Borden Papers.
[27] Canada, H. of C. Debates, 1923, IV, 4001.
[28] Sir Clifford Sifton to J. W. Dafoe, Nov. 19, 1920, Dafoe Papers.

absurd, and am convinced that Canada's true policy right now is to develop her resources and to leave European questions such as the Bessarabian frontier &c to our Imperial statesmen and the trained experts of Downing Street."[29] His successor, O. D. Skelton, while holding "the trained experts of Downing Street" in somewhat lesser regard, was no more sympathetic to the Geneva experiment. Mackenzie King, as his official biographer remarks, "was the type of uplifter who might have been expected to give the League his full and enthusiastic support," but his attitude towards the League in its formative years "was one of studied neglect."[30] In the 1930's this was to develop into an attitude of profound hostility, especially after the "Riddell incident" of November 1935. W. A. Riddell, the Canadian Permanent Delegate at Geneva, left in some perplexity as a consequence of the General Election a few days earlier, proposed on his own initiative the imposition of certain sanctions against Italy, and in the brief period until his action was repudiated by the Canadian government, set Canada's policy upon a course it had never before taken. In his published recollection of this celebrated episode, Dr. Riddell attributes his repudiation partly to the fact that the Prime Minister and the Under Secretary of State for External Affairs were at the time out of the country, leaving the Department of External Affairs in charge of "two French Canadians," Ernest Lapointe and Laurent Beaudry. On reporting to Mackenzie King in Ottawa, Dr. Riddell writes, he found him, "as always, most gracious," while Lapointe seemed "cold, critical and overbearing."[31] But beneath a mask of practiced cordiality King was no less angered than Lapointe, probably more so, by Riddell's initiative. A Canadian newspaperman has recorded an interview with the Prime Minister soon after the event:

Had a few words with Mr. King re the Italo-Ethiopian settlement and he spoke with surprising frankness. I never knew before Mr. King's general attitude towards the League and foreign affairs. King complained angrily about Dr. Riddell's gasoline [sic], steel and coal proposal. "I am certainly going to give him a good spanking", was the way he put it. . . . He said that excessive idealism in politics should be avoided. Canada's policy, he believed, should be dictated by considerations of geographical location and population. After all we are but 10 millions on the north end of a

[29] Entry for Dec. 11, 1920, Pope Papers (P.A.C.).
[30] Dawson, op. cit., p. 403.
[31] W. A. Riddell, World Security by Conference (Toronto, 1947), p. 140.

continent and we should not strive to over-play our part . . . He is very dubious about foreign commitments, and, also, about getting into the League too deeply. He said that the only real difference of opinion he had ever had with Lapointe was with regard to Canada's acceptance of the presidency of the League Assembly [in 1925]. He had opposed it on the ground that it would stimulate League thought in Canada, tend to lead us more deeply into League affairs and, possibly, foreign commitments.[32]

"We should not strive to over-play our part." This theme was henceforth to be heard in nearly all of the Prime Minister's infrequent public statements on the European crisis until the outbreak of war, a refrain in praise of diffidence. "After all, . . . there is such a thing as a sense of proportion in international affairs," he said in the House of Commons in February 1936. "Do hon. members think that it is Canada's role at Geneva to attempt to regulate a European war . . .?" If he had not disavowed Riddell's proposal, "the whole of Europe might have been aflame today."[33] A few days later he added: "Our country is being drawn into international situations to a degree that I myself think is alarming."[34] Within a fortnight Hitler was to invade the Rhineland.

3. The Law and the Jungle

If distrust of European politics contributed to isolationist sentiment in Canada in the years between the wars, it also helped to thwart understanding of what was happening to Europe during the deepening crisis of the later 1930's. With a very few exceptions, notably J. W. Dafoe,[35] Canadians did not recognize Fascist Italy and Nazi Germany for what they were. Totalitarianism was thought to be merely an aggravation of that *malaise* from which Europe traditionally suffered; there was little if any suspicion that it might be a distinctively twentieth-century phenomenon arising from the tensions and insecurities of twentieth-century man. The fascist appa-

[32] Grant Dexter to J. W. Dafoe, Dec. 17, 1935, Dafoe Papers.
[33] Canada, *H. of C. Debates*, 1936, I, 97, 98.
[34] Quoted in F. H. Soward, *et al.*, *Canada in World Affairs: The Pre-War Years* (Toronto, 1941), p. 23.
[35] Of whose newspaper it was well remarked that "what the *Free Press* thinks today, Western Canada will think tomorrow and the intelligent part of Eastern Canada will think a few years hence." Frank H. Underhill, "J. W. Dafoe," *Canadian Forum*, XIII (Oct. 1932), 22.

rition was no new menace for which the old responses would no longer suffice, but a rebirth of the intrigues, the rivalries, the nationalisms of prewar European diplomacy. Thus it required no special explanation; created no new problems; needed no exceptional precautions.

A significant section of the Canadian public was indeed disposed to view fascism in its Mediterranean setting not merely without alarm but with undisguised approval. The lofty sentiments of Fascist doctrine elaborated by Mussolini's publicists, with their apotheosis of order, discipline, family, nation, their pseudo-syndicalist remedies for industrial unrest, gained powerful support among the elite of French Canada. "The work of Mussolini and of the Fascist Party finds among a certain number of my compatriots admirers," remarked Mr. Paul Gouin in 1938. "They have the same attitude towards the corporative movement of Salazar. . . . We may ask ourselves if it would not be to the advantage of our Province and of Canada to borrow what is best in these different formulae, while naturally avoiding their excesses."[36] Few French-speaking Canadians saw anything for adverse comment in the description of General Franco's forces offered by the newly appointed Papal Delegate to Canada and Newfoundland as that "army of heroes, justly called Christ's militia,"[37] any more than they resented the valedictory pronounced by Maxime Raymond in the House of Commons on the occasion of the departure of the Mackenzie-Papineau Brigade: "This, I admit, does not give me any sorrow; it will rid us of these undesirable people, provided they do not return here."[38] If there was no emulation in French Canada of General O'Duffy's Blueshirts, who went from Eire to fight in Spain for Franco, it was due not to want of sympathy for the Nationalist cause but to the even stronger hold of isolationism.

National Socialism was something else again. No religious or ideological link could bind Quebec to a regime which had so soon and so obviously singled out the Catholic Church for brutal destruction. But diagnosis of the Nazi movement was hindered in Canada by the magnitude of domestic crisis and by the isolationist tradition. Events in Germany were consistently misconstrued as a nationalist revival of

[36] Quoted in Henri Saint-Denis, "Fascism in Quebec: A False Alarm," *Revue de l'université d'Ottawa*, Jan. 1939, p. 4. See also "S," "Embryo Fascism in Quebec," *Foreign Affairs*, XVI (April 1938), 454-466.
[37] *Le Devoir* (Montreal), July 14, 1938.
[38] Canada, *H. of C. Debates*, 1937, I, 910.

the conventional type, distinguished, perhaps, by the odd fanaticism of its leaders, by the strut and swagger of its rank and file, but for all that a movement which might be comprehended in traditional terms, appeased and contained by traditional methods. When Hitler entered the Rhineland there was aroused among English-speaking Canadians little of the emotion produced by Mussolini's attack on Ethiopia. On the contrary, there was a widely held conviction that in reoccupying the demilitarized zone Hitler was only avenging the wrongs of Versailles, taking possession of what rightfully belonged to Germany. Why shouldn't a man walk into his own backyard? With the significant exception of Dafoe's *Free Press,* nearly all Canadian newspapers urged, on March 9, 1936, a sympathetic understanding of Hitler's position. "Canadians who do not allow themselves to be swayed by a personal dislike for Hitler and his unpleasant colleagues," wrote the editor of the Vancouver *Sun,* "will feel a measure of sympathy for this new attitude of the German people. . . . Canada is only a spectator. There are not enough moral principles at stake to induce her to become otherwise. . . . Whatever morality lies in the scales seems to be, this time, on Germany's side of the balance." "After eighteen years," the Edmonton *Bulletin* observed, "Europe can afford to restore Germany to full standing in the concert of nations." "Nothing can ever be gained," argued the editor of the Montreal *Gazette,* "by persistently treating Germany as though she were national enemy No. 1 in perpetuity. It would likewise be dangerous and futile to regard Adolf Hitler in no other light than as one whose designs are wilfully antagonistic to forces that hate war."

It is possible that had Canada been represented in Germany by a diplomat of insight and influence, a less reassuring image of National Socialism would have reached its government and people. As it was, the Canadian government, having no diplomatic mission at Berlin, necessarily relied on whatever Whitehall might select for its instruction from the despatches of Sir Nevile Henderson—despatches which conveyed a sadly erroneous interpretation of Nazi policy.[39] This unhelpful source was supplemented by the assessment of the Canadian High Commissioner at London, so closely associated with the group

[39] During the Munich crisis in the fall of 1938, Henderson wrote of "Hitler's own love for peace, dislike of dead Germans and hesitation of risking his regime on a gambler's throw." Quoted in Felix Gilbert, "Two British Ambassadors: Perth and Henderson," in Gordon A. Craig and Felix Gilbert, *The Diplomats, 1919-1939* (Princeton, 1953), p. 543.

which moved with such great and disastrous effect between Cliveden, Printing House Square, and Downing Street that nothing he learned from its members seems likely to have provided a useful corrective to the misleading despatches passed on by the Dominions Office. "Walked about the grounds in the forenoon with Vincent Massey, talking politics," wrote Thomas Jones in his diary on June 7, 1936. "I begged him to stress the urgency of dealing with Germany and not to wait upon France."[40]

But the most misleading impression was derived more directly. In 1937 Mackenzie King decided to go from the Imperial Conference to Germany. There he met and talked with Hitler and other leading personalities of the Third Reich. It was not a wholly useful confrontation. It is true that King did not allow so unique an opportunity to pass without stressing in Berlin what he felt unable to disclose in London, namely, that in the event of "a war of aggression, nothing in the world would keep the Canadian people from being at the side of Britain."[41] Heeded or not heeded, this message was at least delivered, and more valuable service could hardly have been rendered. But its value was diminished by the way in which the Canadian Prime Minister fell victim to the Führer's remarkable capacity for mesmerizing his visitors. "There is no doubt that Hitler had a power of fascinating men," Mr. Churchill wrote in his memoirs; and added the sage advice: "Unless the terms are equal, it is better to keep away."[42] As between the Prime Minister of Canada and the perpetrator of the Nazi *Schrechlichkeit* the terms were far from equal. The extent of Hitler's advantage may be measured by the opinions with which King returned to Canada. According to Mr. Bruce Hutchison, to whom he related them soon afterward, King found Hitler

a simple sort of peasant, not very intelligent and no serious danger to anyone . . . obsessed with the recovery of neighboring territory inhabited by Germans, a natural feeling. When he had brought these territories into the Reich . . . he would be satisfied . . . he would not risk a large war.

[40] Thomas Jones, *A Diary with Letters, 1931-1950* (London, 1954), p. 218. See also Thomas Jones to Lady Grigg, March 8, 1936, *ibid.*, pp. 179-181; *The History of 'The Times': The 150th Anniversary and Beyond, 1912-1948*, Part II, 1921-1948 (London, 1952), p. 938; John Evelyn Wrench, *Geoffrey Dawson and Our Times* (London, 1955), p. 369.

[41] Canada, *H. of C. Debates*, 1944, VI, 6275.

[42] Winston S. Churchill, *The Second World War*, I: *The Gathering Storm* (London, 1949), p. 250.

His ambitions were centered entirely in Germany and the narrow irreden-
tist regions beside it.   For this reason [there would be] . . . no early
trouble in Europe. . . .[43]

And to the Canadian people Mackenzie King declared, three weeks
after his talks with the German leaders:

Despite every appearance to the contrary, I believe the nations of Europe
have a better understanding of each other's problems to-day than they
have had for some years past.   Moreover, despite all appearances, they are
prepared, I believe, in an effort to work out a solution, to co-operate to a
greater degree than has been the case for a long while. . . . Of this I am
certain . . . that neither the governments nor the peoples of any of the
countries I have visited desire war, or view the possibility of war between
each other, as other than likely to end in self-destruction, and the destruction of European civilization itself.[44]

That the destruction of European civilization was precisely the object
of the man he had so recently talked with in the Reichskanzlei was
a thought unlikely to have crossed the mind of the Canadian Prime
Minister; for, as was remarked of him in a different connection, "Mr.
King never quite got it into his head during his economic studies at
Toronto and Harvard that our civilization is dominated by carnivo-
rous animals."[45]

4. Empire and Reich

In 1923 the Prime Minister of Canada had protested vigorously
and decisively against the Imperial Conference "assuming the rights
of a cabinet in the determination of foreign policy . . . , expressing
approval of the present [British] Government's foreign policy . . . ,
trying to shape the affairs of Europe."[46]   By 1937 Mackenzie King's
suspicions of "Downing Street domination" had been sufficiently
allayed to allow him to do what he had never done before—to
endorse at an Imperial Conference a united Commonwealth policy
on international affairs.   As it happened, the policy for which the
Dominions offered their collective approval and support was the ill-

[43] Bruce Hutchison, *The Incredible Canadian* (Toronto, 1953), p. 226.
[44] Speech given over the National Network of the Canadian Broadcasting Corporation, July 19, 1937.
[45] Frank H. Underhill, "The Close of an Era: Twenty-five Years of Mr. Mackenzie King," *Canadian Forum*, XXIV (Sept., 1944), 125.
[46] Quoted in Dawson, *op. cit.*, p. 474.

fated policy of appeasement. ". . . the settlement of differences that may arise between nations," asserted the section of the *Proceedings* of the Conference dealing with foreign affairs, ". . . should be sought by methods of co-operation, joint enquiry and conciliation . . . differences of political creed should be no obstacle to friendly relations between Governments and countries . . . nothing would be more damaging to the hopes of international appeasement than the division, real or apparent, of the world into opposing groups."[47] These sentiments, which, as Professor Mansergh rightly remarks, are "hardly consistent with the dignity of a great Commonwealth confronted with the shameless aggression of European tyrants unmatched for their cruelty and faithlessness since the Dark Ages,"[48] continued to be uttered by Mackenzie King during the interval between the end of the Conference and the beginning of war. For the first time since becoming Prime Minister in 1921 he found himself able to pay public tribute to "the unremitting care and anxiety which those responsible for the foreign policy of Britain have devoted to their task"; he spoke of "their strong and determined effort to establish peace."[49] This was followed by a series of press statements in praise of British policy. When the news of the proposed mission to Berchtesgaden reached him, Mackenzie King announced that he had "conveyed to Mr. Neville Chamberlain the deep satisfaction with which my colleagues and I have learned that his proposal for a personal conference with Herr Hitler . . . has been agreed to" and described "this far-seeing and truly noble action on the part of Mr. Chamberlain" as "emphatically the right step." A further statement issued after the British Cabinet's decision to support the principle of self-determination for Sudeten Germans referred to the "courage and vision" displayed by the Government of the United Kingdom in seeking "to avert recourse to force by finding a peaceful and agreed solution of the present clash of interests in Central Europe." Following Chamberlain's radio address of September 27, 1938 ("How horrible, fantastic, incredible it is that we should be digging trenches and fitting gas-masks because of a quarrel in a far away country"), Mackenzie King proclaimed the Canadian government's "complete accord with the statement Mr. Chamberlain has made to the world today." Word

[47] Imperial Conference, 1937, *Summary of Proceedings,* pp. 14, 16.
[48] Mansergh, *op. cit.,* p. 89.
[49] Canada, *H. of C. Debates,* 1938, III, 3182.

of the impending visit to Munich called forth the most ecstatic endorsement of all:

The heart of Canada is rejoicing tonight at the success which has crowned your unremitting efforts for peace. . . . My colleagues in the Government join with me in unbounded admiration at the service you have rendered mankind. . . . On the very brink of chaos, with passions flaming, and armies marching, the voice of Reason has found a way out of the conflict.

It may be safely assumed that these utterances were carefully noted and transmitted to Berlin by the German Consul General at Ottawa, Herr Windels; and to the extent that the disordered diplomatic apparatus at the Wilhelmstrasse was capable of bringing them to the attention of the Führer they can only have reinforced his belief that the British Empire was too weak and too craven to oppose his plans for the subjugation of Eastern Europe as a prelude to the destruction of the West. Appeasement, the only foreign policy on which the Commonwealth has ever been in substantial agreement, thus came close to accomplishing its ruin. Offered in the hope of peace, it led it straight to war.

Yet while Mackenzie King had by 1937 become able to support Britain's appeasement of Germany, his earlier fear of centralized control persisted in the realm of defense. All attempts on the part of the United Kingdom to co-operate militarily and industrially with Canada in advance of the outbreak of war were rebuffed. "From 1936 onwards," the official history of the Royal Air Force recalls reproachfully, "Canada, which enjoyed an ideal strategic position and a convenient proximity to the vast industrial resources of the United States, was repeatedly approached [with the request to make facilities available for the training of pilots and aircrew]; but the Canadians, largely for domestic reasons, felt unable to accept our proposals. . . ."[50] At the Imperial Conference of 1937 "the principal Supply Officers' Committee tried to pilot through . . . an agreement with Canada about wartime supplies of bauxite and aluminium," but failed largely because of Canadian opposition.[51] In the summer of 1938 the Board of Trade entered into negotiations with the Canadian government to make provision in advance of war for adequate supplies of certain

[50] Denis Richards, *Royal Air Force 1939-1945*, I: *The Fight at Odds* (London, 1953), pp. 72-73.
[51] *History of the Second World War*, United Kingdom Civil Series, M. M. Postan, *British War Production* (London, 1952), p. 89.

strategic materials; but Ottawa being unwilling to assume such commitments, by September 1939 "virtually no preparations had been made for the war-time purchase of raw materials in North America."[52] Munitions fared little better; with the exception of a contract for Bren machine guns, nothing was done by the Canadian government to assist United Kingdom defense officials in their effort to stimulate the manufacture of arms in the overseas Dominions.[53]

It is thus a major irony of Commonwealth history that Canadian influence on British policy was at this stage brought to bear in the worst of all possible ways. In external policy, as Professor Mansergh observes, "what was most of all required was not a greater consensus of Commonwealth opinion but the more vigourous expression of independent and conflicting opinion";[54] in defense policy what was most of all required was a united effort to create a deterrent of imperial power. The Canadian response was to voice with unaccustomed fervor approval of British statecraft while resisting Britain's efforts to improve the Empire's defenses. While "No evidence so far published suggests that doubts about the unity of the Commonwealth were a major factor in encouraging German aggression,"[55] a firmer signification of the Commonwealth's will to resist might have given Hitler pause; in any event the opportunity was both too good and too rare to be squandered. Certain it is that a fuller measure of defense preparation would have made his defeat less costly and precarious. The margin of superiority with which Britain faced the Axis in the summer of 1940 remained excruciatingly narrow. Had the R.A.F. failed, for want of aircraft or of pilots, to deflect and defeat the Luftwaffe, would not those responsible for Canadian policy during the prewar years have to share the blame?

5. Statecraft and Unity

On January 20, 1937, the Canadian Prime Minister spoke in confidence to a meeting of his parliamentary supporters. He urged them to reject the views of Mr. Arthur Meighen, the Conservative

[52] *History of the Second World War,* United Kingdom Civil Series, J. Hurstfield, *The Control of Raw Materials* (London, 1955), p. 254.
[53] See *History of the Second World War,* United Kingdom Civil Series, H. Duncan Hall, *North American Supply* (London, 1954).
[54] Nicholas Mansergh, *Survey of British Commonwealth Affairs: Problems of Wartime Co-operation and Post-War Change, 1939-1952* (London, 1958), p. 17.
[55] Mansergh, *Survey . . . : Problems of External Policy,* p. 446.

Leader in the Senate, "that the amount in the [defense] estimates was not enough, that we were concerned with the defence of the Empire as a whole; that the first line of our defence was the Empire's boundaries." Equally he urged them to reject the alternative offered by J. S. Woodsworth, the leader of the socialist group in the House of Commons, who, he said, "would do nothing at all" for defense. "The safe policy is the middle course between these two views. . . . Let us explain that policy to our people and let us above all strive at all times to keep Canada *united*."[56] This insistence upon the over-riding importance of national unity appears again and again in Mackenzie King's statements on external policy during the years immediately preceding World War II. It served to explain his reluctance to participate in projects or pronouncements likely to deter potential aggressors. To do so, as he remarked in the House of Commons on May 24, 1938, "would bring out deep and in some cases fundamental differences of opinion, [and] would lead to a further strain upon the unity of a country already strained by economic depression and other consequences of the last war and its aftermath."[57] Of the wisdom of this policy its architect betrayed neither doubt nor misgiving, and believed it fully vindicated by events. On September 8, 1939, he spoke as follows in the House of Commons:

I have made it, therefore, the supreme endeavour of my leadership of my party, and my leadership of the government of this country, to let no hasty or premature threat or pronouncement create mistrust and divisions between the different elements that compose the population of our vast dominion, so that when the moment of decision came all should so see the issue itself that our national effort might be marked by unity of purpose, of heart and of endeavour.[58]

It is a matter for debate whether this "supreme endeavour" was not altogether too restricted. Politics is the art of the possible. But how much was possible during the years before the war? More, perhaps, than the Prime Minister of Canada allowed the nation, or himself, to believe. Never was Mackenzie King more satisfied than when enunciating the dictum that his country was difficult to govern. It was, and is, difficult to govern, in the sense that government is at all times and in all places an exacting and complicated craft. Com-

[56] Quoted in Stacey, *op. cit.*, p. 14.
[57] Canada, *H. of C. Debates*, 1938, III, 3184.
[58] Canada, *H. of C. Debates*, 1939 (Special War Session), I, 25.

pared to the ordeals which nearly every twentieth-century nation has undergone—destruction and occupation in war, civil conflict, malevolent and scouring tyrannies—Canadians might consider their situation extraordinarily favorable. Nor were those wearying comparisons between the continent of the undefended frontier and "the continent which cannot run itself" too easily reconciled with plaintive references to exceptional domestic difficulties invoked to justify inaction. So much harping upon the need for unity and the obstacles in its path exaggerated the degree of internal discord, just as repetition of the difficulties encountered in governing the country obscured the fact that it was a good deal less difficult to govern than most. Was it not misleading "to emphasize the precariousness of Canada's export markets, but not the value of her exports; to speak of regional and cultural tensions within but not of the growing sense of unity; of the conflicting pulls of geography and history to which indeed every 'settled' country is subject, but not of the immense strength of Canada's position in the heart of the English-speaking world"?[59] When the history of these years is set out in detail, many of the portents of disunity in the Dominion will be seen to have been greatly overdrawn. For example, it is commonly believed that had the United Kingdom gone to war over Czechoslovakia in September 1938, the C.C.F. (Socialist) party in Canada would have demanded a policy of neutrality. But Professor McNaught has discovered that "correspondence in the Saskatchewan C.C.F. files . . . leaves no doubt that the C.C.F. leaders who defeated the Woodsworth-Farmer neutrality motion in the emergency National Council meeting in [September] 1939 had concluded at least as early as September, 1938, that 'it is already decided that if Britain declares war, Canada must accept the situation.' "[60]

A direct result of reducing Canadian policy to the lowest common denominator of public agreement was the condition of the nation's defenses, "utterly inadequate," as the official historian of the Canadian Army observes, "by comparison with the scale of the coming emergency."[61] Another harmful consequence was the effect upon United Kingdom policy. Just as the Canadian government seized with alacrity upon stress and strain in the Dominion's domestic affairs as an excuse for passivity in all external policies save that of appease-

[59] Mansergh, *Survey . . . : Problems of External Policy*, p. 111.
[60] McNaught, *op. cit.*, p. 54 n. 40.
[61] Stacey, *op. cit.*, p. 35.

ment, so the British government fastened upon the difficulties of members of the overseas Commonwealth to justify its own cautious conduct. Disunity in the Dominions plays a major part in the arguments of apologists for Britain's prewar policy. "The fact remains that the Commonwealth Governments were unwilling to go to war on the issue of Czechoslovakia," a former British Foreign Secretary has written of that period. "Dominion opinion was at the time overwhelmingly against a world war. This opposition was continually in our minds. Time after time we were reminded of it, either by the High Commissioners in London, or by Malcolm MacDonald, the Secretary of State for the Dominions. As early as March 18, 1938 we had been told that South Africa and Canada would not join us in a war to prevent certain Germans from rejoining their Fatherland."[62]   While "The actual policy Mr. Chamberlain followed in September 1938 owed little or nothing to dominion inspiration,"[63] there can be no doubt that dispiriting responses from the Dominions were used by him to discourage those within the British Cabinet who urged a less cowardly posture in the face of German threats.[64]   In Canada's case their effect was the more damaging for their misrepresentation of the real intention of its government. For had war broken out at the time of Munich, the Prime Minister "was prepared to call Parliament within two weeks and submit to it a policy of Canadian participation. . . . The Cabinet was unanimous."[65]

Over half a century ago the French historian André Siegfried had noted the timidity of Canada's political leaders. "They seem . . . ," he wrote, "to stand in fear of great movements of public opinion, and to seek to lull them rather than to encourage them and bring them to political fruition."[66]   It will be observed that Canadian political leadership at the time of M. Siegfried's examination was provided by Sir Wilfrid Laurier; and that it was upon Sir Wilfrid Laurier's leadership that Mackenzie King had faithfully modeled his own. "You do Sir Wilfrid Laurier an injustice in regarding him as an opportunist," King had written a friend during the controversy over naval policy in 1909. "He is other than that. . . . We have had no man in Canada who has done as much to reconcile differences of

---

[62] Viscount Templewood, *Nine Troubled Years* (London, 1954), p. 323.
[63] Mansergh, *Survey . . . : Problems of External Policy*, p. 439.
[64] See *Old Men Forget: The Autobiography of Duff Cooper* (London, 1954), pp. 239-240.
[65] "Back Stage in Ottawa," *Maclean's Magazine*, II (Nov. 1, 1938).
[66] André Siegfried, *The Race Question in Canada* (London, 1907), p. 142.

race and creed and to make of the people one nation. If he hesitates to go to the length that some desire, it is because he does not wish disruption and believes that a united progressive Canada is a more valuable asset to the Empire, and will be so through time, than a Canada divided in opinion, or professing an obligation it is not in a position to meet."[67] But hesitation for the sake of unity was not the inevitable response of all Canadian leaders to the tensions of their plural society; there were those to whom its tensions the more insistently demanded bold and imaginative statecraft. "In our Dominion where sections abound," Mr. Arthur Meighen once declared, "a Dominion of races, of classes and of creeds, of many languages and many origins, there are times when no Prime Minister can be true to his trust to the nation he has sworn to serve, save at the temporary sacrifice of the party he is appointed to lead."[68] Faithfully practicing this doctrine, Mr. Meighen was compelled to retire from public life. Mackenzie King's very different concept of political leadership, no less faithfully practiced and resulting in political longevity only once surpassed in the history of the Commonwealth, must face a very different kind of criticism. It "would have been improved," his official biographer has conceded,

had he been more venturesome and more willing to offer forthright advice to the nation. King's tactics enabled him to secure and retain office—the indispensable first step. But King, too frequently, stopped right there; and because he was reluctant to press on and try to realize some independent conception of the national interest, his policies slipped into the mire of pure expediency. King was always reluctant to venture into the unknown. He avoided taking risks, and he would postpone action, if by so doing he could ensure a greater degree of safety. He dreaded unnecessary discussion which might lead to disagreement and even threaten the existing party solidarity on which the whole security of his position rested. He was not prepared to use his own power extensively in an effort to modify the character and scope of those common elements on which he sought to base his policy. He was too willing at times to yield his own judgment when confronted with opposing opinion. He was slow to admit that he had a duty as leader to exert a moderate pressure in the direction in which he believed the country should move.[69]

[67] Mackenzie King to Lord Stanhope, July 23, 1909. Quoted in Dawson, *op. cit.*, p. 215.

[68] Arthur Meighen, *Unrevised and Unrepented: Debating Speeches and Others* (Toronto, 1949), p. 319.

[69] Dawson, *op. cit.*, pp. 417-418.

This verdict is the more severe coming as it does from "one who is in general sympathy with Mr. King and his work and career."[70]   There is no part of Mackenzie King's long responsibility for Canadian affairs to which it may with more justice be applied than to his conduct of external policy during that "low dishonest decade" when the world lay "defenceless under the night" and so few free men in power dared to "show an affirming flame."

[70] *Ibid.*, p. viii.

5

The Treaty Power in Canada

David R. Deener

Over the past few decades, Canada's constitutional arrangements for the exercise of the treaty power have become the target of loud and sometimes bitter complaint. "Canada's capacity to participate in the life of the international community of states remains grossly impeded," declares one critic.[1] Another commentator adds: "Canada has already its 'Bricker Amendment.'"[2] Even the Canadian government itself has entered the lists with the cautious remark that the constitutional basis for the treaty power "has in recent years given rise to some difficulty."[3]

The particular difficulty referred to is a constitutional situation which "does not permit the Federal Parliament to implement certain types of treaties without concurrent legislative action on the part of the Canadian Provinces."[4] Now, whether this situation does in fact "grossly" impede the Canadian nation in international affairs is perhaps a debatable proposition,[5] but it certainly does operate to present concrete problems to Canadian treaty-makers and their foreign counterparts as well as to executive and judicial officials concerned with carrying out Canada's international obligations. These problems in their historical, constitutional, and international legal aspects will be

[1] G. J. Szablowski, "Creation and Implementation of Treaties in Canada," *Canadian Bar Review*, XXXIV (Jan., 1956), 59.

[2] Maxwell Cohen, "Some International Law Problems of Interest to Canada and to Canadian Lawyers," *Canadian Bar Review*, XXXIII (April, 1955), 396.

[3] "Memorandum of 21 July 1952 from the Government of Canada," in United Nations Legislative Series, *Laws and Practices Concerning the Conclusion of Treaties* (New York, 1953); ST/LEG/Ser. B/3 (Dec., 1952), p. 24.

[4] *Ibid.*

[5] See, for example, the views of F. H. Soward, "External Affairs and Canadian Federalism," in A. R. M. Lower, F. R. Scott, *et al.*, *Evolving Canadian Federalism* (Durham, N. C., 1958), pp. 149-160.

the main points of emphasis in this discussion of Canada's treaty power.

1. Evolution of the Treaty Power

The Original Design. "Canada has very few statutory provisions relating to the exercise of the treaty-making power. The rules followed, so far as they can be ascertained, are for the most part founded on unwritten custom."[6] This statement by the Canadian government serves to underline the importance of broad principle and historical precedent in the evolution of Canada's treaty power. Indeed, the background of principle and precedent was of first importance in determining the stipulations regarding treaties placed in the British North America Act of 1867.

Two sets of principles relevant to the treaty power were operative in the framing of the British North America Act. The first set derived from Lord Durham's formula for colonial autonomy. Under this formula, certain matters of "imperial" concern (and the regulation of foreign relations was among these) would remain with the mother country. Otherwise, "internal legislation" so-called was to be left in the hands of the colonial government.

True, by 1867 Lord Durham's formula had already begun to break down and certain matters earlier presumed to be "imperial" were in fact being turned over to responsible colonial governments. But this was not yet so in the case of foreign relations; in 1867 the making of treaties was still the province of the Imperial Government. Hence, the British North America Act was simply silent on this point, since treaties affecting Canada were to be negotiated by the London government.

The Act of 1867 was not silent, however, in regard to the implementation of treaties. In fact the only provision of the Act specifically dealing with the treaty power relates to implementation. This is Section 132 which provides as follows:

The Parliament and Government of Canada shall have all powers necessary or proper for performing the obligations of Canada or of any Province thereof, as part of the British Empire, towards Foreign Countries, arising under Treaties between the Empire and such Foreign Countries.

[6] "Memorandum of 21 July 1952 from the Government of Canada," document cited n. 3, *supra*, p. 24.

At first glance, Section 132 might be reckoned a departure from Lord Durham's formula, since treaty implementation could with some logic be deemed to fall within the regulation of foreign relations, a subject classed as imperial in Durham's *Report*. On the other hand, there was also logic and above all precedent for placing treaty implementation with the colonial government. As an example of precedent, the Canadian-American Reciprocity Treaty of 1854 may be mentioned. Article 5 of the Reciprocity Treaty provided that it was to go into effect when legislative action had been taken not only by the Imperial Parliament but also by the several parliaments of the British North American provinces. Furthermore, when the Act of 1867 was being debated in the British House of Commons, a member, referring to the unsuccessful attempt to renew the Reciprocity Treaty, remarked upon the "enormous advantage" to be gained from Section 132. Had the renewal attempt succeeded, the member pointed out, the treaty would have had to have been submitted to all of the British North American parliaments, instead of just one as contemplated by Section 132.[7]

Section 132 is also related to the second set of principles that entered into the original design of Canada's treaty power. These are the principles of parliamentary government and of federalism which the framers of the British North America Act sought to combine. However, these two constitutional principles, at least as developed in England and the United States respectively, tend to take somewhat different approaches to the treaty power. In the English tradition, the parliamentary principle proceeds upon a "dualistic" view of the treaty power. That is, to use the words of a Canadian jurist, a "treaty is deemed a contract or convention between . . . two nations and does not become a part of the law of the land unless by express Act of the legislative body."[8] But in the United States the federal principle takes a "monistic" approach to the treaty power. That is, again to borrow from a Canadian jurist, "treaties duly made are 'the supreme law of the land' equally with Acts of Congress duly

[7] The incident in the British House of Commons is taken from Szablowski, *op. cit.*, p. 37. An opinion of United States Attorney-General Caleb Cushing on the Reciprocity Treaty may be noted here. He advised that the President of United States could not proclaim the Treaty until all of the parliaments mentioned in Art. 5 had taken appropriate action; 6 *Official Opinions of the Attorneys General of the U. S.* 748 (1854).

[8] Wright J., in *Re Arrow River and Tributaries Slide and Boom Co., Ltd.,* [1931] 1, D. L. R. 260, 266.

passed."[9] In Section 132, the framers of the British North America Act adopted the "dualistic" rather than the "monistic" approach to the treaty power.

Toward External Sovereignty. In original design, the British North America Act contemplated that treaties would be made in London but implemented in Ottawa. This transatlantic division of function was gradually to change as Canada moved toward external sovereignty and independence. In fact, the path from colonial to Commonwealth and independent status is well marked with the steps by which Ottawa assumed control over the making of treaties affecting Canada. Several important steps were taken before 1900. These included the association of Canadian representatives in treaty negotiations, acknowledgment of the right of Canada and other self-governing colonies to adhere separately to commercial treaties, and, later, to withdraw separately. After 1900 the pace of events quickened. The Convention of 1907 with France was negotiated entirely by Canadian representatives, although submitted for approval to British authorities. Canada and other Dominions sent representatives to various international conferences, including the International Radio-Telegraph Conference of 1912 and the International Conference on Safety of Life at Sea of 1913-1914. These were followed by the Versailles Peace Treaty Conference of 1919 and the milepost of Dominion participation therein.

Then came the Halibut Fisheries Convention of 1923 between Canada and the United States and the Imperial Conference of the same year. The Fisheries Convention was negotiated between Ottawa and Washington and signed only by Canadian and United States representatives, to the exclusion of a British representative. The Imperial Conference of 1923 has been described as simply "sanctioning the precedent" established in the Halibut Fisheries Convention.[10] The Conference gave recognition to the fact that Canada and the other Dominions were free from Imperial control at least in commercial treaty-making when it reached agreement that:

It is desirable that no treaty should be negotiated by any of the Governments of the Empire without due consideration of its possible effect on other

[9] Lamont J., in *Arrow River and Tributaries Slide and Boom Co., Ltd.,* v. *Pigeon Timber Co., Ltd.,* [1932] S. C. R. 495, 510.
[10] This is the phrase of Robert B. Stewart, *Treaty Relations of the British Commonwealth of Nations* (New York, 1939), p. 75.

parts of the Empire, or, if circumstances so demand, on the Empire as a whole.[11]

The advances toward external sovereignty since 1923 are familiar as landmarks in the emergence of the British Commonwealth. They would include the Imperial Conference of 1926, the appointment of a Canadian Minister to Washington in 1927, the Statute of Westminster of 1931, and the heightened diplomatic activity of Commonwealth members resulting from World War II.[12] One further development with respect to Canada remains to be mentioned. This is the issuance of the Letters Patent of 1947 by which the British Crown delegated to the Governor General-in-Council "all powers . . . lawfully belonging to Us in respect of Canada."[13] By virtue of this delegation, all of the incidents of treaty-making, including the issuance of full powers and the act of ratification, can be, and in fact regularly are, taken in Ottawa without reference to London.

With the attainment of external independence, the original design of Canada's treaty power was altered in respect of negotiation. Now that Canada was to conclude treaties on its own, questions concerning the original arrangements for implementation also arose. Section 132 of the British North America Act clearly conferred upon the Canadian Parliament the power to implement treaties made by the Imperial Government in London. But did the Section apply only to Imperial treaties? or would it encompass also treaties made by Canada on its own? The answers to these questions were to be hammered out in the forge of the constitutional politics of Canadian federalism.

2. Federalism and the Treaty Power

As events have worked out, the final answers to date regarding Section 132 and treaty implementation have not been given by Canadian courts but by the Judicial Committee of the Privy Council in England.[14] In one of the first cases to arise after Canada had assumed

[11] Cmd. 1987.

[12] The development of Dominion control over treaty-making is treated in excellent fashion in R. B. Stewart, op. cit., which covers fully the phases relating to political, extradition, and technical treaties not touched upon in the brief summary given here. Dr. Stewart's work also treats in detail changes in the formalities of issuing full powers and of ratifications to the date of the book (1939).

[13] Revised Statutes, 1952, VI, 306.

[14] Appeals in civil cases to the Privy Council were not abolished by Canada until

control over its treaty-making in the 1920's, it appeared that the Privy Council might be moving toward an interpretation of Section 132 so as to cover treaties made by Canada. In the *Radio Communications Case*, Viscount Dunedin said of the Radio Telegraphic Convention of 1927 that, "though agreeing that the Convention was not such a treaty as is defined in s. 132, their Lordships think that it comes to the same thing."[15] In the *Labour Conventions Case*, however, the Privy Council took a somewhat different tack. Lord Atkin, spokesman for the Judicial Committee, advised that obligations under these Conventions "are not obligations of Canada as part of the British Empire, but of Canada, by virtue of her new status as an international person, and do not arise under a treaty between the British Empire and foreign countries."[16] Accordingly, in the view of the Privy Council, Section 132 was not applicable to treaties negotiated by Canada on her own.

Obviously, this holding as to Section 132 left open the whole question of how treaties made by Canada were to be implemented, since under the "dualistic" view of treaty power, legislative action generally is required to make a treaty part of the law of the land. Lord Atkin did not neglect this question. In the federal scheme for distribution of legislative powers in the British North America Act, so Lord Atkin opined,

there is no such thing as treaty legislation as such. The distribution is based on classes of subjects: and as a treaty deals with a particular class of subjects so will the legislative power of performing it be ascertained.[17]

In more specific terms, Lord Atkin pointed out that,

if in the exercise of her new functions derived from her new international status she [Canada] incurs obligations they must, so far as legislation be concerned when they deal with provincial classes of subjects, be dealt with by the totality of powers, in other words by co-operation between the Dominion and the Provinces.[18]

1949; see The Supreme Court Act, 1949, 13 Geo. VI, c. 37 and *Attorney-General for Ontario v. Attorney-General for Canada*, [1947] A. C. 127.
   [15] [1932] A. C. 304, 312.
   [16] [1937] 1 D. L. R. 673, 680.
   [17] *Ibid.*, 681-682.
   [18] *Ibid.*, 683-684. Lord Atkin went on to say: "While the ship of state now sails on larger ventures and into foreign waters she still retains the water-tight compartments which are an essential part of her original structure." The view of the Canadian Constitution expressed in this statement is sometimes referred to as Lord Atkin's "water-tight compartment" interpretation of Canadian federalism.

Thus, suggesting that the power to implement treaties negotiated by Canada is dependent upon the federal division of powers between the central government and the provinces, the Privy Council in a sense tended to transform the "dualistic" principle of the British North America Act into a "pluralistic" approach. Furthermore, since Section 92 of the Act of 1867 assigns to the provinces the subject of "Property and civil rights in the Province," the decision provides a good argument for those who want to extend provincial jurisdiction to the increasingly wide variety of matters dealt with in treaties. It was probably to be expected, then, that the *Labour Conventions Case* would come in for its full share of criticism. Professor Hendry has declared: "Historical reason and logic gives no firm foundation for the restrictive interpretation placed on this clause [Section 132] by the Privy Council. Indeed the Section has now been relegated to cover a situation which no longer exists."[19] Professor Scott has added: "A major constitutional limitation in international affairs was imposed on the Canadian nation in the very decade in which she finally achieved full national status."[20]

There is, however, another way to view the *Labour Conventions Case,* as something else besides an aberrant caprice of the Privy Council. In retrospect the case is but one incident, albeit of highest import, in the ceaseless struggle for power between center and provinces. And the provincialistic interpretation of the treaty power adopted in the case was not the invention of the Judicial Committee. On the contrary, the provincialistic interpretation had been urged much earlier in the federal struggle, well before Canada had begun to make treaties on its own. In 1908 British Columbia argued, unsuccessfully it may be noted, that its Immigration Act permitting exclusion of Japanese was enforceable notwithstanding a treaty between Great Britain and Japan stipulating that Japanese were free to enter the Dominion and an act of the Dominion Parliament sanctioning said treaty.[21] Again, in the early 1920's, British Columbia attempted by statute to restrict the employment of Japanese, but again was unsuccessful in contending for the validity of its law in the face of the Japanese Treaty of 1913 and Dominion legislation sanc-

---

[19] James McLeod Hendry, *Treaties and Federal Constitutions* (Washington, 1955), p. 33.

[20] F. R. Scott, "Centralization and Decentralization in Canadian Federalism," *Canadian Bar Review,* XXIX (Dec., 1951), 1114.

[21] *In re Nakane and Okazake,* [1908] 13 B.C.R. 370.

tioning the Treaty.[22]   A few years later the Crown obtained a conviction of one Stuart for having in his possession two teal ducks in contravention of a Dominion statute implementing the Migratory Birds Convention of 1916 with the United States.   In the appeal proceedings, the Attorney-General of Manitoba entered to argue that Section 132 could not give the Dominion jurisdiction over matters assigned to the provinces by Section 92 of British North America Act.   He suggested a distinction between live ducks which came within Dominion jurisdiction and dead ducks which fell to the provinces, but the Court saw little merit in this mortician's approach to the federal division of power.[23]   In all of these cases, it perhaps should be emphasized, an Imperial Treaty was involved and there was no question but that Section 132 was operative.

The provincialistic interpretation of the treaty power was to find more success when carried to the courts by another route.   In 1920 the Minister of Justice advised the Dominion Cabinet that several draft labor conventions would require provincial legislative action for their implementation.[24]   This advice was in effect substantiated by the Supreme Court in 1925 when it replied to a question referred to it that the subject matter of a draft labor convention regulating the hours of labor was "generally within the competence of the legislatures of the provinces."[25]   The final prelude to the *Labour Conventions Case* was the decision of the Canadian Supreme Court when the case was before it.   The highest court of Canada could not bring itself to reject the provincialistic interpretation, dividing 3 to 3 on the issue.[26]

Thus, when the *Labour Conventions Case* reached the Privy Council, that body had before it a provincialistic interpretation of the treaty power which was of some historical standing, which the highest

---

[22] *In re Employment of Aliens*, [1922] 63 S.C.R. 293.   The Treaty in Art. 1 provided for most-favored-national treatment in respect of industries, callings, and professions.

[23] *The King v. Stuart*, [1925] 1 D.L.R. 12.   This case bears a close analogy to Missouri v. Holland, 252 U.S. 416 (1920), in which legislation enacted by the United States Congress to implement the same Migratory Birds Convention was upheld as constitutional, and, therefore, was held to override conflicting state enactments.

[24] See Soward, "External Affairs and Canadian Federalism," *op. cit.*, pp. 133-134. Note that this advice was given before the Imperial Conference of 1923 and that the treaty involved was the Versailles Treaty under which there was no clear commitment on the part of Canada to implement by Dominion legislation any and all conventions produced by the International Labor Conferences.

[25] [1925] S.C.R. 505, 512.

[26] [1936] S.C.R. 461.

court of Canada had not repudiated, and which was in line with some earlier Privy Council decisions construing the federal scheme for distribution of power in favor of provincial over Dominion power.[27] Still, in the *Labour Case,* the Judicial Committee sharply distinguished its own most recent pronouncements on the treaty power, namely, the *Radio Communications Case* and the *Aeronautics Case,*[28] and this departure, so to speak, from the earlier decisions has led to some speculation regarding the effect of the individual views of the members who comprised the board in 1937. For one thing, the membership had changed radically over the board which had decided the earlier cases. And Lord Wright, who sat on the 1937 board, has strongly intimated that he "dissented" from the opinion of Lord Atkin.[29] It has been suggested that Lord Atkin's views were shared by Lord Thankerton and Lord Wright's by Lord Macmillan, leaving the casting vote to Sir Sidney Rowlatt, a "taxation judge," reported to have "sat throughout the 1937 hearings in his overcoat making neither note or comment."[30]

There is, then, the "fascinating, but disturbing, possibility" that chance and the luck of judicial assignment played a heavy role in determining the outcome of the leading decision thus far on Canada's treaty power. But the decision nonetheless stands and is the constitutional source of many of Canada's current treaty problems, to which attention may now turn.

3. Treaty Problems and the Labour Conventions Case

The "pluralistic-provincialistic" interpretation of the treaty power suggested in the *Labour Conventions Case* obviously creates problems of treaty implementation. But it also leads to complications on

[27] For discussion of the Council's decisions on the federal distribution of powers generally, see F. R. Scott, *op. cit.,* n. 20; A.R.M. Lower, F. R. Scott *et al., Evolving Canadian Federalism* (Durham, N. C., 1958); Edward McWhinney, *Judicial Review in the English-Speaking World* (Toronto, 1956), chap. iv and the numerous references contained therein.

[28] [1932] A.C. 54; also 304.

[29] The intimation is given in a tribute paid to Sir Lyman Duff by Lord Wright, "Rt. Hon. Sir Lyman Poore Duff, G.C.M.G. 1865-1955," *Canadian Bar Review,* XXXIII (Dec., 1955), 1123-1129. It may be mentioned that no "dissenting opinions" are issued by the Privy Council, since its "opinion" is tendered as advice to the Crown which ought not receive conflicting advice.

[30] As suggested by B. J. MacKinnon in a letter, *Canadian Bar Review,* XXXIV (Jan., 1956), 116-117.

the negotiating side, a consequence that the Canadian government has taken pains to make quite clear:

To avoid the difficulty which might arise if provincial legislation, required for the fulfilment of an international obligation, were refused, prior consultations are had, and agreements reached, with the Provinces before Canada enters into international agreements. This makes it difficult for Canada to enter into some international conventions such as the proposed Covenants on Human Rights and Fundamental Freedoms without the inclusion of a federal state clause.[31]

Much of the criticism leveled against Canada's treaty power since 1937 has not really been directed so much at the constitutional difficulties encountered in implementation, as against the consequences of these difficulties, particularly the failure to adhere to various multilateral international conventions and otherwise to participate in the activities of international organizations in a manner deemed desirable by the critics.[32] But the consequences of Canada's implementation difficulties for ordinary bilateral treaties should not be overlooked. Bilateral instruments deal with a wide range of matters, many of which fall within the classes of subjects denominated as provincial in the British North America Act. And there is reason to believe that the Canadian government has preferred not to conclude certain kinds of treaties, such as consular conventions, rather than run the risks likely to be encountered in their implementation.

Another point related to the "pluralistic-provincialistic" concept of the treaty power merits brief attention. It involves an extension of the concept from treaty implementation to treaty negotiation. If the legislative power to implement treaties is distributed between center and provinces, why not also the power to conclude treaties? The Canadian provinces are not sovereign states, of course, and not much real support is likely to be found for the proposition that the provinces possess a treaty-making power in respect of items contained in Section 92 of the British North America Act, but the recent case of the *Attorney General for Ontario v. Scott* has some bearing on the

[31] "Memorandum of 21 July 1952 from the Government of Canada," document cited n. 3 *supra*, p. 25.

[32] The pleading of constitutional difficulties to explain or excuse Canada's failure to take certain international actions has been described by Professor James Eayrs as hiding "its head in constitutional sands." See his "Canadian Federalism and the United Nations," *Canadian Journal of Economics and Political Science*, XVI (May, 1950), 172-183, esp. p. 180.

subject. The case concerned a provisional maintenance order obtained in England and proceedings for its confirmation under the Reciprocal Enforcement of Maintenance Orders Act of Ontario. The argument was offered against the arrangement that it was "in effect, a treaty to which the province has no authority to become a party." The Supreme Court of Canada, however, denied this contention and upheld the reciprocal arrangements.[33] That such reciprocal arrangements might permit a province to do what otherwise would be accomplished by a treaty is, of course, obvious.

A lot has happened since 1937, and the question arises whether any constitutional developments have occurred which might affect the "pluralistic-provincialistic" pattern of the treaty power as established in the *Labour Conventions Case*.

One development given prominent mention is the abolition in 1949 of appeals in civil cases to the Privy Council. Those desirous of mitigating the effects of the *Labour Conventions Case* have expressed the hope that Canadian judges will hereafter interpret the British North America Act liberally as a "constitution" rather than narrowly as a "statute." That the Canadian Supreme Court would flatly reverse the *Labour Conventions Case* and reinterpret Section 132 as applying to treaties made by Canada is, however, an exceedingly remote possibility. A second course urged is a return to the path begun in the *Radio Communications Case*. Under this proposed course, the Court would deem legislation necessary to implement treaties as falling within Section 91 of the British North America Act and the power of the central Parliament to make laws for "the peace, order, and good government" of Canada. While there are some serious obstacles to adopting this course in *carte blanche* fashion,[34] the recent case of *Johanneson v. Rural Municipality of Saint Paul* suggests that it might be done in a piecemeal manner. This case in-

---

[33] [1956] S.C.R. 137, 142. The Scotts had been married in Scotland and had come to Canada to live. They had separated and Mrs. Scott had returned with their children to England. She had applied for and received from an English court a provisional order requiring Mr. Scott to pay certain sums weekly for the use of herself and the children.

[34] One difficulty is the wording of Section 91. The Dominion is assigned the power to make laws "for the peace, order, and good government of Canada, *in relation to all matters not coming within the classes of subjects by this Act assigned exclusively to the legislatures of the Provinces.*" The adoption of a *carte blanche* course would require a virtual erasure of the exception (italicized here for emphasis) insofar as treaty legislation is concerned.

volved a Manitoba statute authorizing municipalities to regulate the location of airports. The earlier *Aeronautics Case* had upheld under Section 132 Dominion legislation passed in 1927 to implement the Convention relating to the regulation of Aerial Navigation of 1919. The Convention of 1919 had been repudiated in 1947 and replaced by later aerial agreements, but the original statute of 1927 remained on the books. Despite the fact that the statute of 1927 did not itself regulate the location of airports, the Supreme Court declared the Manitoba statute to be *ultra vires*. Justice Locke stated that the "whole subject of aeronautics lies within the field assigned to Parliament as a matter affecting the peace, order and good government of Canada."[35]

Two further developments relating to judicial interpretation remain to be mentioned. One is the case of *Re Drummond Wren* in which the Ontario High Court ruled a racially restrictive covenant to be contrary to public policy. To ascertain public policy, the Court surveyed among other things the provisions of the United Nations Charter.[36] Somewhat similar interpretive possibilities have been suggested in connection with the proposed Canadian Bill of Rights, introduced by the Diefenbaker Government in 1958.[37] The bill contains language similar to phrases found in the United Nations Charter and the Declaration of Human Rights. The suggestion is that the Bill of Rights might enable Canadian courts to make use of the central ideas in the Declaration, "without of course, admitting that any or all the matters in the Declaration have a specific or positive legal status as such."[38] What these developments hint at is that treaties even when unimplemented may still have some effect in determining cases coming before the courts.

In addition to judicial amendment and interpretation, there is always the possibility of direct formal amendment of the British North America Act. Although amendment of the Act specifically in

---

[35] [1952] S.C.R. 292, 328.
[36] [1945] 4 D.L.R. 674. The Court did not, of course, apply the Charter as law of the land. See C. B. Bourne's comment, "International Law—Unimplemented Treaties—Their Effect on Municipal Law—Public Policy," *Canadian Bar Review*, XXIX (Nov., 1951), 1969-1974. In *Re Noble and Wolf*, [1948] 4 D.L.R. 123, [1949] 4 D.L.R. 375, [1951] S.C.R. 64, also involving a restrictive covenant, considerable doubt was cast on the *Wren Case*.
[37] Bill C-60, 24th Parl., 1st Sess. (1958).
[38] This is the suggestion of Professor Maxwell Cohen; see his comment, *Canadian Bar Review*, XXXVII (March, 1959), 228-233, esp. p. 232.

relation to the treaty power has been urged,[39] little in that direction appears likely in the immediate offing.[40] On the other hand, specific amendments giving the Dominion Parliament powers over unemployment insurance[41] and old age pensions[42] have passed, and these amendments will naturally facilitate exercise of the treaty power in relation to these matters.

A last development of note is the invocation by the central government of certain special powers it possesses. Parliament may, for example, declare a work or works to be for the general advantage of Canada and thereby acquire competence. This procedure was used in the Atomic Energy Control Act of 1946, with special reference being made to the purpose of enabling Canada to participate effectively in measures of international control.[43] When, however, the Atomic Energy Control Act came under attack in the courts, it was sustained under the general powers of Parliament to make laws for "the peace, order and good government" of Canada.[44] Another power to be mentioned is that of the central Parliament to enact criminal law; in a proper case, this power could be used to implement treaty commitments.

It is doubtful whether the developments and possibilities mentioned above have as yet effected any serious alteration in the "pluralistic-provincialistic" pattern of the treaty power set forth in the *Labour Conventions Case.* They do suggest that Lord Atkin's "water-tight compartments" may have sprung a few leaks, and, moreover, that a reconsideration of the 1937 Privy Council decision by the Supreme Court of Canada is a distinct possibility in the future. The *Labour Conventions Case,* notwithstanding, when the interests involved are great enough, as in the St. Lawrence River project, the provinces and the Dominion can co-operate to make effective use of the treaty power.[45]

[39] The Rowell-Sirois Commission recommended that the "Dominion should be empowered to implement any labour conventions of the International Labour Organization. It should be understood, however, that we do not here make any recommendations with respect to treaties in general." *Report of the Royal Commission on Dominion-Provincial Relations* (1940), Bk. II, p. 49.

[40] The final procedure for amending the Canadian Constitution without recourse to action by the Imperial Parliament has yet to be worked out.

[41] The British North America Act, 1940, 3-4 George VI, c. 36.

[42] The British North America Act, 1951, 14-15 George VI, c. 32.

[43] *Revised Statutes,* 1952, c. 11.

[44] *Pronto Uranium Mines Ltd. v. Ontario Labour Relations Board,* [1956] 5 D.L.R. (2d) 342.

[45] See the International Rapids Power Development Act, 1951, *Revised Statutes,*

4. More Treaty Problems

Not all Canadian treaty problems result from the "pluralistic-provincialistic" approach to the treaty power. In the first place, the "pluralistic-provincialistic" approach does not apply to all Canadian treaties. The subject matter of many treaties will fall so obviously within Dominion jurisdiction that no question will arise as to the power of the federal Parliament to implement them. Also, there are numerous treaties made before Canada assumed full control over the treaty power and still in force, and there is no authoritative holding, despite exclamations to the contrary,[46] to the effect that Section 132 is not operative in regard to them. For these treaties, the original "dualistic" design of the treaty power obtains.

The possibility of non-performance of treaty obligations through legislative inaction is a problem by no means peculiar to the "pluralistic-provincialistic" approach. It is a distinct possibility in the "dualistic" approach, too, as reference to situations involving the Webster-Ashburton Treaty and the Canadian-American Boundary Waters Treaty of 1909 will illustrate.

The Webster-Ashburton Treaty contains a provision, Article 2, that specified boundary rivers shall be "free and open" to citizens of both Canada and the United States. Two separate cases arose in Canadian courts involving improvements made on boundary rivers by private companies, for the use of which tolls were exacted. In the first case, the improvements and tolls had been authorized by the legislature of Minnesota; in the other case, the authorization had been given by the legislature of Ontario. In the Minnesota case, the Canadian court stated that the act of the Minnesota legislature was invalid since it was in conflict with the Webster-Ashburton Treaty which in the United States was part of the law of the land.[47] In the Ontario case, however, while admitting that the provincial act was contrary to the provisions of the treaty, the Canadian court con-

---

1952, c. 157, and the agreement between the Government of Canada and the Government of the Province of Ontario contained in the schedule thereto.

[46] Thus, Professor Hendry's statement that Section 132 has been "relegated to cover a situation which no longer exists" (*op. cit.*, p. 33) and Professor Scott's cry that "Empire treaties have vanished with the Empire" (*op. cit.*, n. 20, p. 1112), are perhaps a little exaggerated.

[47] *Rainy Lake River Boom Corporation v. Rainy River Lumber Co.*, [1912] 6 D.L.R. 401.

cluded that the provincial law was nonetheless valid since the treaty had not been implemented by either the Dominion or Imperial Parliaments.[48]   Thus, as Canadian courts saw it, under the "monistic" principle operative in the United States, the treaty of itself worked to invalidate a conflicting state law; but under the "dualistic" principle operative in Canada, the same treaty of itself had no effect at all on a conflicting provincial act.

A similar situation has arisen in the current Columbia River controversy. Article 2 of the 1909 Boundary Waters Treaty provides that persons injured by diversion or interference of waters on either side of the boundary are entitled to the same rights and remedies as if the injury took place in the country where the diversion occurred. In the case of diversion of the Columbia River in British Columbia, injurious to downstream American users, the question arises of what rights and remedies they might have under British Columbia law. It has been pointed out that British Columbia law in effect provides rights and remedies only to water users licensed by the province. Hence a downstream American injured by diversion in British Columbia could not gain relief in British Columbia courts, so opinion runs, since he would not be a user licensed by British Columbia.[49]   Here, again, is evidence of the effect of the "dualistic" principle followed in Canada, for what appears to be lacking is, as Professor Cohen suggests, a Dominion statute properly implementing the Treaty of 1909 under Section 132.[50]

Another problem concerns the submission of treaties to Parliament. It is related to a principle of parliamentary government since, in the English tradition, the conclusion of treaties is considered to be solely an executive act. The Canadian government takes the position that it is under no constitutional obligation to submit treaties to Parliament prior to ratification.[51] The Canadian House of Commons, however, in its resolution of June 21, 1926, approving the recommendations of the Imperial Conference of 1923, went on record to

[48] *Arrow River and Tributaries Slide and Boom Co. Ltd. v. Pigeon Timber Co., Ltd.,* [1932] S.C.R. 495.

[49] See Charles E. Martin, "The Diversion of Columbia River Waters," *Proceedings of the American Society of International Law, 1957,* pp. 2-8.

[50] Maxwell Cohen, "Some Legal and Policy Aspects of the Columbia River Disputes," *Canadian Bar Review,* XXXVI (March, 1958), 37-38. It may be noted that in *Francis v. the Queen,* [1956] S.C.R. 618, implementing legislation for Art. 3 of the Jay Treaty of 1794 was found lacking.

[51] "Memorandum of 21 July 1952 from the Government of Canada," document cited n. 3 *supra,* p. 24.

the effect that the approval of Parliament should be secured before treaties affecting Canada are ratified or treaties or agreements involving military or economic sanctions are accepted.[52] As matters stand at the present, virtually all treaties and other international agreements are laid before Parliament in one way or another, but in only a relatively few cases is parliamentary approval obtained prior to their entering into force.

5. The Treaty Power in Perspective

"No other federal state in the world is so restricted," declares Professor Scott in speaking of Canada and the treaty power.[53] Many other commentators have emphasized the limitations on Canada's treaty capacity. By way of conclusion, then, a brief comparison of Canada's treaty power with that of the United States seems appropriate.[54]

In formal constitutional terms, Canada's treaty power does indeed appear severely restricted in comparison to that of the United States. The underlying "dualistic" approach of the British North America Act as modified by the "pluralistic-provincialistic" outlook of the Labour Conventions Case tends to anchor the treaty power to the basic federal distribution of power, a distribution made primarily for internal rather than international purposes. The "monistic" principle operative in the United States coupled with the implications of Missouri v. Holland not only tends to divorce the treaty power from the internal federal distribution, but also, when a treaty is involved, to enlarge, to "internationalize," the internal distribution as well. There are, however, some factors which work to loosen the strictures of the Canadian constitutional arrangement on the one hand, and to constrict the operation of the American system, on the other.

In the United States, a distinction between self-executing and non-self-executing treaties has developed.[55] For the category of treaties deemed non-self-executing, this distinction tends to transform

[52] The resolution is reproduced in *Replies from Governments to Questionnaires of the International Law Commission*, UN doc. A/CN. 4/19 (1950).

[53] Scott, *op. cit.*, n. 20, p. 1114.

[54] "For more elaborate comparison, see James M. Hendry, *op. cit.*, and J. P. Nettl, "The Treaty Enforcement Power in Federal Constitutions," *Canadian Bar Review*, XXVIII (Dec., 1950), 1051-1070.

[55] See Alona E. Evans, "Some Aspects of the Problem of Self-Executing Treaties," *Proceedings of the American Society of International Law, 1951*, pp. 66-75.

the "monistic" approach of the Constitution into a "dualistic" approach since legislation will be required for their implementation. In Canada a distinction between ordinary treaties and what might be termed "prerogative" treaties has appeared. As for "prerogative" treaties so-called, it has been said that they "do not require legislative confirmation," even though they "purport to change existing law or restrict the future action of the legislature."[56] In the case of "prerogative" treaties, then, the "dualistic" and even the "pluralistic-provincialistic" approach of the British North American Act presumably does not present limitations.[57]

Nor can political factors be neglected. Despite Canada's constitutional incapacities in regard to labor conventions, her record of actual ratifications compares favorably with that of the United States. And the "monistic" principle has not caused the United States to desist in seeking federal-state clauses in certain instances. In fact, with respect to some multilateral conventions of broad social import, Canada and the United States have both refused ratification, although for opposite reasons: Canada because of inability to implement; the United States because of automatic implementation if it did ratify.

In broader political terms, both federal systems have witnessed in the twentieth century strong movements based on state and provincial rights to place limits on the treaty power. These movements have produced results in Canada and near-results in the United States that have been the source of considerable annoyance to many international lawyers. Yet to see these movements only as destructive of international law and as obstacles to effective international order is to overlook, perhaps, the significance of constitutional government in the conduct of international relations. The essence of constitutional government is restraint on power. The treaty power in the twentieth century is not what it was in the nineteenth. Modern treaties touch virtually every aspect of modern life. The logic of constitutionalism contains no exemption for a power of such magnitude, and the experience of both Canada and the United States attests to the practical validity of that logic. Perhaps the greatest lesson taught by the experience of the two North American federal systems is that the federal principle will be utilized to establish a

[56] Per Rand J., in *Francis v. the Queen*, [1956] S.C.R. 618, 625, 626.
[57] See *Gallant v. West*, [1955] 1 D.L.R. 441; *Municipality of St. John v. Fraser-Brace Corp.*, [1958] S.C.R. 263.

balance between the internal desires for restraints on the treaty process and the external need for effective treaty power. Canadian history of the past two decades reflects the strong pressure in behalf of a greater treaty power, when the balance had been tipped too far in the direction of restraint. United States experience of the same period reflects strong pressures for internal restraints when the long-standing constitutional balance seemed in the eyes of certain important domestic groups to be weighed too heavily in favor of the treaty power.

6

Le Canada Francais: Du Provincialisme a l'Internationalisme

Gérard Bergeron

Note liminaire: Ce petit travail ne vise pas à établir une *thèse.* Il se borne à indiquer les caractères plausibles d'une *hypothèse* nouvelle. En fait, l'hypothèse est invérifiable actuellement. Les processus historiques, qu'elle présente sous son éclairage propre, sont trop récents, leur ambivalence actuelle est trop accusée pour qu'on n'accorde pas son dernier mot à l'Evénement sans doute inconnu et peut-être imprévisible.

D'ailleurs, ce travail est beaucoup trop court pour un sujet de cette ampleur. Il reste à souhaiter que d'autres (comme certains jeunes sociologues et historiens du Canada français que nous connaissons personnellement) reprendront peut-être cette hypothèse, moins pour en décanter la part de vérité qu'elle contient, que pour contribuer au renouvellement de l'attirail des idées reçues, et donc, de toute (et fausse) sécurité sur le Canada français. Il nous semble que l'idée reçue de l'isolement culturel et politique des Canadiens français doit être actuellement revisée.

L'auteur procède à ce début de révision. Il le fait à sa manière. De par sa formation et ses centres majeurs d'intérêt qui se sont toujours axés sur l'étude des relations internationales, l'auteur a pu être amené à maximiser les facteurs et indices qui rendent l'hypothèse vraisemblable. C'est un risque normal de l'opération pour la raison générale que la proposition d'une hypothèse nouvelle peut, autant que pour l'établissement d'une thèse complète, amener à "forcer" les faits. Mais aussi pour la raison particulière que l'auteur, abordant son sujet sous l'angle de sa spécialité, voit, initialement et davantage, le phénomène "Canada français" dans ses dimensions internationales que sous l'angle de ses structures et de ses dynamismes internes. Cette dernière optique a toujours été celle de ceux qui ont écrit sur le Canada français, à l'exception peut-être de certains analystes étrangers, tel un Siegfried (et encore le faisaient-ils selon un caractère de généralité et d'imprécision, pour ne pas dire d'impressionisme, qui étaient bien loin d'être toujours significatifs).

Commençant un cours au Collège de France, Jules Michelet disait: "Messieurs l'Angleterre est une île. Vous en savez maintenant autant que moi sur son histoire." La boutade de Michelet soulignait fortement l'inspiration et la tradition insulaires de toute la politique britannique.

J'éprouve la tentation de commencer cet article par la boutade désenchantée, et si souvent citée, de Sir Wilfrid Laurier: "La province de Quebec n'a pas d'opinions; elle n'a que des sentiments." A quoi il conviendrait d'ajouter: "Vous en savez maintenant autant que quiconque sur son histoire." Mais cette phrase n'aurait pas l'à propos qu'elle avait dans la citation de Michelet. Pourquoi? Parce qu'elle n'exprime pas une donnée objective, indiscutable comme "L'Angleterre est une île. . . ." Dire des Canadiens-français qu'ils n'ont pas d'idées en politique, mais seulement des sentiments, c'est qualifier des attitudes psychologiques, déterminer des dispositions subjectives. C'est interpréter.

Il vaudrait mieux se servir de la même métaphore que l'historien romantique: "Le Canada français est une île au milieu d'un océan anglo-saxon,"—comme la Roumanie est une île de latinité au sein d'un univers slave.

Cela n'apprend pas tout sur l'histoire du Canada français. Mais c'est donner une bonne idée de ses perspectives.

Le Canada français, c'est aussi un important segment du Canada tout court (environ 30% de la population totale). De ce point de vue, c'est beaucoup plus qu'une "île." Mais quelles que soient les sphères d'extension des "grands touts" (nord-américain ou, restrictivement, canadien), où l'on localise le Canada français, il conserve toujours une homogénéité optima et une pleine individualité. Il est le groupe minoritaire le plus vivace, différent et cohérent de l'Amérique du Nord. De fait, il a été, est, et sera sans doute pour longtemps encore, le seul viable. D'où son intérêt unique comme objet d'analyse.

1.

Politiquement, le Canada français correspond assez exactement à la province de Québec.[1] Doù un caractère marqué de "provincialisme" dans la vie politique et culturelle du Canada français. Mais ce n'est pas là un caractère spécifique. On sait l'importance du *sectionnalisme* aux Etats-Unis, du *régionalisme*[2] au Canada. On pourrait même voir l'Amérique du Nord composée d'une série de provincialismes juxtaposées: contre les impératifs nord-sud de la géographie, on a établi artificiellement des unités politico-économiques selon l'axe est-ouest, aboutissant ainsi à des quadrillages provinciaux, mi-naturels, mi-artificiels.

Le Canada français est un *cas* parmi les divers provincialismes nord-américains. Un *cas* plus accusé que d'autres, non seulement à cause de cette quasi concordance avec les cadres territoriaux d'un état *provincial,* mais surtout à cause d'une communauté ethnique culturelle et religieuse dont l'homogénéité et la permanence détonnent si curieusement dans le continent du *melting pot.* Il s'ensuit chez les Canadiens-français—même chez ceux qui se prétendent dégagés des oeillères d'un nationalisme étroit, stérile ou irréel—un involontaire ethnocentrisme, ou mieux, un *provincialo-centrisme.* C'est fatal peut-être, normal certainement.

Mais d'autre part, à l'ère des fusées intercontinentales et des satellites artificiels, les Canadiens commencent à prendre conscience pour la première fois en temps de "paix"[3] des grandes réalités internationales et singulièrement de l'inconfortable double voisinage des U.S.A. et de l'U.R.S.S. Les Canadiens d'expression anglaise qui donnent au Canada sa configuration principale, ont, par le sentiment d'appartenir à la famille britannique mondiale, toujours eu le sentiment actif—même à l'époque coloniale—de participer à un internationalisme de fait. Les Canadiens-français, eux, n'ont jamais eu jusqu'à une date récente le sentiment de devoir s'ouvrir largement à la vie internationale. Et même: *ils n'ont pas encore pris une conscience active de la réalité étatique canadienne.*

[1] Si, culturellement, cette seule province n'épuise pas toute la réalité canadienne française, tout comme la réalité culturelle québecoise n'est pas exclusivement canadienne-française.

[2] De l'Ouest, des Maritimes, etc.

[3] Si l'on peut dire . . .

D'emblée, ils sont à faire *le grand écart entre le provincialisme d'hier et l'internationalisme d'aujourd'hui sans le passage intermédiaire du nationalisme pancanadien.*[4] C'est pensons-nous, l'observation fondamentale que nous commande notre sujet. Imbus, faits d'esprit provincial (et conservés tels, dans leur individualité profonde, par cet esprit), les Canadiens-français ne semblent pas avoir été *médiatisés* par le sentiment d'appartenance au grand Etat canadien avant d'être forcés d'accéder à la vie internationale.

Du provincial à l'international sans passer par le national. Ou de la *partie* aux relations entre *touts,* sans passer par le *tout* qui englobe la partie. C'est là un hiatus culturel aussi large (et qui se serait produit beaucoup plus rapidement) que celui du passage d'une société rurale-agricole à celui d'une société urbaine-industrielle. Ce dernier phénomène a attiré l'attention studieuse de la première génération de *social scientists* que le Canada français se soit donné.[5] Personne encore n'a semblé avoir eu conscience du premier phénomène.

Le trait marquant du nationalisme canadien-français a été de s'exprimer politiquement en un *provincialisme* s'opposant moins aux Canadiens d'autres origines qu'à l'impérialisme britannique, donc à un surnationalisme d'origine extérieure. Depuis 200 ans, les articulations maîtresses de l'histoire de ce nationalisme se situent aux grandes phases de l'émancipation constitutionelle du Canada. Et, dans la mesure où ce nationalisme s'opposait à celui des Canadiens d'expression anglaise, c'était pour leur reprocher un loyalisme britannique trop fervent ou même une connivence impérialiste. Le nationalisme pan-canadien d'un Bourassa faisait exception à ce provincialisme national, nationalisme basique des Canadiens-français.

---

[4] L'auteur ne se dissimule pas les difficultés méthodologiques qu'il soulève, sans les résoudre, par l'emploi de concepts comme "provincialisme" (distingué et partiellement opposé à celui de "nationalisme" canadien-français) et "internationalisme" (opposé à celui de "nationalisme" canadien-français) et "internationalisme" (opposé à "nationalisme" et "supernationalisme" et distingué d' "universalisme"). Ce serait précisément l'objet d'un travail plus satisfaisant, que nous souhaitions en note liminaire, de préciser ces concepts, de leur donner, au minimum, une validité opératoire, et, à son défaut, de les remplacer par d'autres.

Mais pour les fins du présent travail, contentons-nous de dire que ces mots auront une valeur plus vulgairement sémantique que proprement conceptuelle. Ajoutons aussi qu'ils ont ici une faible densité idéologique, surtout si on dégage—dans la mesure où la chose est possible ou permise—le contenu idéologique des faits, attitudes et sentiments collectifs qui le supportent et l'expriment, ainsi que des comportements individuels qui réfléchissent ou conditionnent ces faits, attitudes et sentiments collectifs.

[5] Cf. Jean-C. Falardeau, ed., *Essais sur le Québec contemporain* (Québec, 1953).

Aussi "l'autre," "l'extérieur" par rapport au Canadien français, c'était l'Anglais, indistinctement celui de Londres ou celui de Toronto ou celui d'Ottawa qui faisait, sur place, la politique impériale. Nos relations internationales étaient des relations intra-impériales, constitutionnelles, des relations de famille, imposées, de raison. Ce n'étaient pas de véritables relations internationales. Elles n'initiaient pas les Canadiens-français à une politique étrangère.

A l'autre point d'angle de ce fameux "triangle nord atlantique,"[6] se trouvent les Etats-Unis. Du Traité de Paris, 1763, à la Déclaration d'Indépendance, 1776, les Canadiens-français firent un bout d'existence commune avec les futurs Américains. Encore numériquement majoritaires au Canada, ils prenaient conscience de la précarité de leur position par rapport à leurs "voisins du sud,"[7] mais ils savaient que, quoiqu'il advint, la métropole les prenait en charge. Ils jouèrent le jeu de la nouvelle métropole impériale, se refusant de se donner de nouveaux maîtres, fussent-ils libérateurs. D'où leur "loyalisme" aux invasions de 1776 et 1812: loyalisme, cependant qu'il conviendrait de ne pas trop sublimer.[8]

Dans l'histoire de ces relations triangulaires, les intérêts canadiens sont pris en charge par l'Angleterre et représentés par elle. Pour un Canadien anglais, qu'il soit plus ou moins teinté de colonialisme, cela représentait un jeu concret d'intérêts réels, au moins pour l'avenir, pour l'avenir d'une grandeur impériale ou d'un hypothétique Canada indépendant. Pour un Canadien-français, pourvu qu'on ne le dépouillât pas de son patrimoine, cela représentait un jeu abstrait et lointain d'intérêts qui, de toute façon, lui seraient extérieurs. Aussi, à chaque rivalité d'intérêts, à chaque marchandage, il est fort heureux de ne pas trop écoper, de n'être pas le seul à faire les frais de l'opération. C'est un spectateur, éventuellement une victime, non un acteur.

Donc, dans ses relations avec la Grande Bretagne, le Canada est dans un réseau de dépendance puis d'indépendance graduelle, mais lente: relations d'ordre constitutionnel, non d'ordre international. Dans ses relations avec les Etats-Unis, le Canada est l'objet, la ma-

---

[6] Cf. John Bartlet Brebner, *North Atlantic Triangle* (New Haven, 1945), et Edgar McInnis, *The Atlantic Triangle and the Cold War* (Toronto, 1959).
[7] Cf. Gustave Lanctôt, Jean Bruchési, *et al.*, *Les Canadiens français et leurs voisins du Sud* (Montréal, Editions Bernard Valiquette et New Haven: Yale University Press, 1941).
[8] Cf. *ibid.*, chap. iii, "Le Québec et les Colonies américaines."

tière, le point de rencontre des rapports, eux décisifs quant à lui,[9] de la Grande Bretagne et des Etats-Unis. Le Canadien français, à qui la grandeur impériale ne dit très exactement rien, non plus qu'une chimérique indépendance complète comme celle des 13 Colonies révoltées, le Canadien français, lui, consacrera tous ses efforts à prendre sa place "provinciale" au sein de ce Canada, construit contre nature et, de toute façon vouée irréversiblement à être à prépondérance anglo-saxonne. Ce provincialisme n'a jamais eu, jusqu'à l'époque récente de la guerre froide, l'idée d'un internationalisme pratique: et même, il n'a jamais fait sa conversion active à un nationalisme pancanadien, si ce n'est que comme à un *statu quo* qui lui est toujours apparu aussi fumeux qu'inévitable.

Mais il faut donner à ce provincialisme sa double dimension, ou mieux sa double présence. Il ne s'affirmait pas seulement dans la politique du gouvernement du Bas-Canada ou, plus tard, de la Province de Québec en ce qu'elle s'opposait à celle de l'autorité centrale ou de l'opinion prépondérante du Canada anglais. Les Canadiens français furent aussi présents et actifs, et de façon presque continue, dans l'élaboration des politiques canadiennes d'ensemble. Comme l'écrivait le professeur Frank H. Underhill:

Ever since the late 1840's, when Responsible Government was put into practice in Canada, members of the French-Canadian group have sat to the right of Mr. Speaker in the Canadian legislature and Parliament, save for ten unhappy years from 1911 to 1921. That is, they have formed part of the government. They have brought it about that no major decision in Canadian policy can be taken without their consent. They have established, in other words, the principle of concurrent majorities. Every French Canadian is a practising John C. Calhoun.[10]

Mais, le fait est notable, quand des Canadiens français assument des responsabilités gouvernementales canadiennes, ils le font toujours comme des espèces de "fondés de pouvoir" de la province française du Canada et, parfois même, de la façon la plus claire au moment où ils s'en défendent le plus. Sans remonter jusqu'à George Etienne Cartier, il apparaît déjà que l'idée directrice des grands leaders cana-

---

[9] "Anglo-American understanding was henceforth to be, if not always acknowledged, the cardinal principle of Canadian foreign policy, for if Great Britain and the United States began to pull in opposite directions the vulnerable Dominion of Canada was bound to be the first casualty." Brebner, *op. cit.*, p. 197.

[10] Frank H. Underhill, *The British Commonwealth* (Durham, N. C., 1956), pp. 25, 26.

diens a toujours été celle-là: un Laurier, un Lapointe, un Saint-Laurent.[11]

Il n'est certes pas facile de démêler la part proprement canadienne française dans l'élaboration d'une politique extérieure commune. Cela impliquerait la possibilité de discerner des points de vue et attitudes spécifiques. Evidemment, il y a des cas clairs: mais ils ne sont pas plus nombreux que 3 ou 4. Dans l'opinion, les journaux, au Parlement, les Canadiens français ont toujours réclamé un drapeau et un hymne national authentiquement canadiens, l'adhésion à l'Union pan-américaine,[12] la présence d'un ambassadeur canadien au Vatican. Par dessus tout en matière de politique militaire, ils ont été anti-conscriptionnistes et anti-participationnistes aux guerres extérieures. De fait, les deux grandes crises de désunion nationale survinrent lors des deux guerres mondiales, alors que la question de la levée en masse des soldats canadiens s'est dramatiquement posée.

Hormis ces questions où il existe un point de vue particulier aux Canadiens français, il faut encore dire que notre jeune[13] politique étrangère a toujours montré un rare degré d'unanimité. La spécificité de la politique étrangère du Canada laissait peu de place à de vives controverses entre partis non plus qu'entre groupes ethniques, sauf sur la question très cruciale de la participation aux guerres extérieures. En fait, on n'épuiserait pas les 5 doigts de la main si l'on comptait les

[11] Il est assez curieux de constater que ces hommes politiques canadiens français ont parfois joué un rôle de premier plan dans la politique étrangère du Canada: Laurier qui, le premier, prend la décision d'envoyer un corps expéditionnaire canadien dans une guerre coloniale de l'Empire Britannique (Transvaal, 1899), Lapointe le signataire du premier traité international du Canada (Halibut Treaty, 1923), St-Laurent, le premier secrétaire aux affaires extérieures après que la fonction ait été détachée de celle de premier ministre (1946). On pourrait aussi mentionner les rôles de premier plan qu'ont joué un Rodolphe Lemieux ou un Raoul Dandurand. James Eayrs, dans ce même volume, rappelle que lors de l'incident Riddell à la Société des Nations en 1935, le principal intéressé, W. A. Riddell, expliquait partiellement le désaveu de son attitude par le gouvernement canadien par le fait que deux Canadiens français, Ernest Lapointe et Laurent Beaudry étaient, au moment de l'incident, responsables par intérim du ministère des affaires extérieures. Cf. page 67.

[12] Devenu depuis l'après-guerre l'Organisation des Etats américains.

[13] Il n'est peut-être pas inopportun de rappeler à des lecteurs américains que le Canada n'est un pays souverain que depuis peu. En 1923, le Canada signait seul, sans la ratification britannique, son premier traité international. Il n'eut son premier représentant diplomatique, hors du Commonwealth, qu'en 1927 avec M. Vincent Massey en poste à Washington. La pleine et officielle indépendance du Canada ne date que de 1931 avec le Statut de Westminster qui entérinait les recommandations du Rapport Balfour en 1926. Enfin, ce n'est que la seconde guerre mondiale qui devait conférer au Canada une véritable "stature" internationale.

cas de divergences sérieuses entre partis en matière de grandes dé-
cisions de politique étrangère.[14]

Mais cela accroît d'autant l'importance *provinciale* du Québec:

But, [comme dit le Professeur Soward] when there was a weak and
divided opposition in Ottawa, the federal government was inclined to keep
a watchful eye on the provincial government and their views, if any, on
foreign policy.

Normally the provinces avoid controversy in this field with the federal
government, except upon immediate economic interests such as wheat, fish,
or power. However, the attitude of one province on broader issues must
always be kept in mind. That province is, of course, Quebec. The cautious attitude displayed towards Quebec exists not only because it sends
seventy-five members to Ottawa, the overwhelming proportion being
almost invariably Liberals, but because Quebec is the home of French-
speaking Canada. Its people, long separated from France, deeply rooted
in the soil and devoted to their language and Church, cannot be expected
to respond in an international crisis as English-speaking Canadians have
often done to what a French-Canadian Cabinet Minister once described as
"the call of the blood." As a people, until recently largely rural and
immersed in the affairs of the parish, they are naturally inclined to isolationism and wary of being drawn into what one of their greatest leaders,
Sir Wilfrid Laurier, described fifty years ago as "the vortex of militarism,
the curse and blight of Europe." When another French-Canadian Prime
Minister, Mr. St. Laurent, angrily inveighed against "the super-men" of
Europe in the debate on the Middle East last winter, he unconsciously
demonstrated a vestigiary survival of that attitude. If an American can
think of the Democratic South (perhaps I should add of pre-Eisenhower
days) often voicing the sentiments of the more isolationist parts of the
Middle West, but in French rather than English, he will find a parallel
to the special role of the province of Quebec in Canadian policy. It is
Quebec more than any other province that necessitates the raising of the
Canadian armed forces by voluntary methods, a method not followed by
any other NATO country with a military establishment. But it cannot be
stressed too much that this attitude would be the same whether Canada
were a federal or a unitary state. The fact is that Canada is and will

[14] Le parti du Crédit social—pour des raisons de doctrine monétaire partisanne—
s'opposa à la participation canadienne aux grands organismes de Bretton Woods en
1944. Le parti CCF critiqua fortement l'insuffisance de la clause de collaboration
économico-sociale (article 2) du Pacte de l'Atlantique Nord. Pendant la crise de
Suez, les Conservateurs firent une lutte acharnée au Ministère Saint-Laurent. Ce fut
certainement un des éléments déterminants de la défaite du parti libéral en 1957.

remain a bicultural state, the product of history and environment and increasingly her people have become accustomed to that phenomenon.[15]

2.

Le Canada est né et s'est maintenu par un refus global: celui d'être annexé par les Etats-Unis. D'autre part, il s'est affirmé par une dissociation graduelle de la Grande-Bretagne. Il est le résultat de deux refus. Il doit son indépendance à deux dépendances. Dans cette lutte pour l'existence, le Canada français a refusé plus tôt et plus fort que le Canada d'expression anglaise. Il avait toujours une avance dans ses refus qui étaient au niveau de l'instinct. C'est le cas classique de tous les groupes minoritaires qui veulent survivre—si cela n'explique pas tout.

Le nationalisme canadien, qui s'analyse de plus en plus en un anti-américanisme—tant sont fortes les multiples pressions américaines sur les divers aspects de la vie canadienne—, est en disponibilité d'opérer une jonction avec le provincialisme nationaliste (ou le nationalisme provincialiste) du Canada français. Il est possible que, dans un avenir imprévisible, ces deux nationalismes aboutiront en un surnationalisme pan-canadien, par où seraient affirmée la double configuration culturelle du Canada et . . . assurée encore provisoirement son indépendance.[16] Si ce jour vient, et quand il viendra, cessera l'écart énorme entre le *provincialisme* de fait qui caractérise toute l'histoire du Canada français et l'aspiration à un *internationalisme* obligé qui le sollicite actuellement. Alors les Canadiens français auront été médiatisés par un *nationalisme pan-canadien*. Ce ne semble pas être le cas actuellement. Mais c'est là faire des projections dans le futur.

Il vaudrait mieux, sans doute, interroger le passé. Pour donner un caractère probant à notre proposition fondamentale, il faudrait que l'étude de l'histoire culturelle du Canada français soit plus riche que les quelques matériaux dont nous pouvons faire état.[17]

[15] F. H. Soward, "External Affairs and Canadian Federalism," in A.R.M. Lower, F. R. Scott, *et al.*, *Evolving Canadian Federalism* (Durham, N. C., 1958), pp. 158-159.

[16] Croit-on qu'advenant une "explication" ultime entre l'U.R.S.S. et les U.S.A., il subsisterait quelque chose de cette "indépendance" canadienne?

[17] Dans la version originale de ce travail pour les fins du *Summer Seminar and Research Group* de Duke University, l'auteur avait retracé en quelque vingt-cinq pages les lignes principales de l'histoire des "relations extérieures" du Canada français, jusqu'à 1914. Il s'agissait là d'un "background material," pouvant servir à la

C'est une histoire curieuse que celle des relations du Canada français et des Etats-Unis après 1763. Au départ il y avait autant de chances que le Canada français s'appuie sur les colonies américaines nouvellement émancipées pour conquérir lui-même sa propre indépendance qu'il y en avait que le Canada français sauvegarde sa survivance ethnico-religieuse en affirmant son obéissance à ses nouveaux maîtres métropolitains. Il y eut deux fortes tentations d'annexion aux Etats-Unis en 1849 et au moment de la construction du Canada moderne en 1867; mais ces tentations furent repoussées comme de mauvais risques.

Les circonstances favorables à une étroite collaboration avec les Etats-Unis étaient qu'après avoir été délaissés par une métropole européenne, les Canadiens français risquaient encore de l'être par la nouvelle ou d'être complètement assimilés ou "déplacés" comme leurs frères acadiens quelques années auparavant. Après que fut apparu viable le nouvel Etat fédéré du sud, il pouvaient y trouver le modèle de leur prochaine émancipation et de leur éventuelle constitution tout en exerçant une douce revanche contre les conquérants. Mais il y avait au bout de ce risque le danger d'une absorption complète. Ils risquaient de se donner de nouveaux maîtres.

Les éléments défavorables étaient non moins importants. Ce sont eux qui l'emportèrent. Même pendant l'époque de leur vie commune, du traité de Paris, 1763, à la Déclaration de l'Indépendance, 1776, les oppositions entre colons anglais et français n'avaient cessé de s'affirmer. Les premiers, barrés par la muraille des Apalaches, avaient été forcés de se livrer au commerce maritime et à la pêche, de cultiver la terre sur place. Cet emprisonnement géographique, joint à une immigration qui avait été autrement importante, avait créé des colonies densément peuplées sur des territoires relativement restreints. La Nouvelle-France, quoique largement ouverte sur l'Atlantique par le golfe Saint-Laurent, exploitait, depuis les origines, la fourrure et, axée sur la voie du Saint-Laurent, était entraînée à toujours pénétrer plus profondément à l'intérieur.

Ainsi, presque continuellement, le territoire de l'une s'étend et la population de l'autre s'augmente, de sorte que chaque fois que la population anglaise veut se donner du champ, elle se heurte à la colonie française qui se hâte de pousser plus loin sa frontière. De là surgissent, d'abord, rivalité et mécon-

---

compréhension de notre sujet, mais qui en débordait les cadres. C'est pourquoi ces pages ne sont pas reproduites ici.

tentement, ensuite empiètement et agression, et finalement guerre et conquête. Cette formule résume, d'étape en étape, toute la suite des relations des colonies anglaises et françaises, du début au traité de Paris de 1763.[18]

Le choc de la première grande guerre mondiale fut la première expérience vraiment internationale du Canada, et des Canadiens français en particulier. Jusque là le Canada prenait des dimensions nord-américaines qui, sauf au sud étaient celles de la géographie naturelle jusqu'aux bords des grands océans: l'idée d'annexionnisme s'éteindra après 1850 et, avec la Confédération de 1867, elle ne sera plus guère, dans le Québec qu'

un argument idéologique dans les mains d'une faction minoritaire et radicale n'ayant aucune perspective d'assumer un jour une responsabilité dans le gouvernement. Elle lui sert surtout à critiquer le ministère en opposant la situation canadienne à la démocratie et à la prospérité américaine. La majorité québecoise ne l'a jamais envisagée comme une éventualité possible, mais l'a toujours repoussée instinctivement et consciemment, parce qu'elle répugne à son premier leitmotiv qui est la survivance canadienne française.[19]

Jusque là le Canada "prenait ses distances" constitutionnelles avec la Grande-Bretagne. Mais la première fois que le Canada est amené à remplir un rôle international d'envergure, il apparaît aux Canadiens français moins un devoir de solidarité humaine au service de la paix que l'accomplissement d'une fatalité impériale. Le Canada français s'estime menacé dans sa substance même; on veut envoyer ses fils à la boucherie! Cette crise de la conscription de 1917, rendue plus grave par mille gaucheries d'un gouvernement spécialement maladroit, allait empêcher la jonction des deux nationalismes canadiens pendant encore une génération.

La chose était d'autant plus regrettable que le Canada, en sa totalité, en était arrivé à la fin de la période, que clôt la première grande guerre, au point d'équilibre économique à peu près parfait dans les relations triangulaires que lui commande son double destin nord-américain et britannique. Ce phénomène fait l'admiration de Brebner:

During this expansive quarter century (1896-1920), the economic triangle of buying and selling, investing and dividend-paying, migration and pro-

[18] Lanctôt, *op. cit.*, p. vii.
[19] *Ibid.*, p. 275.

duction, into which Great Britain, the United States, and Canada poured their efforts, became the mightiest thing of its kind on earth and seemed destined to remain so. Individualism was still practically unbridled, so that competition was the order of the day, but the three areas proved to be complementary in so many ways that they cooperated in spite of themselves.[20]

Dans la période de l'entre-deux guerres, la politique étrangère du Canada fut par-dessus tout conditionnée par la nécessité de refaire, puis de consolider, enfin, de ne pas défaire la précaire unité nationale. Dans une première période qui va jusqu'au statut de Westminster de 1931, le Canada français n'a pas de point de vue tellement différent de celui du groupe majoritaire en politique étrangère. Ou plutôt, il l'approuve dans la mesure où s'affirme un nationalisme pan-canadien dans les affairs internationales, qui apparaît, dès le sortir de la guerre, à la Conférence de Versailles, à la Société des Nations, à la Conférence navale de Washington. C'est là le début d'un internationalisme pratique qui apparaît l'heureuse négation de l'impérialisme britannique traditionnel. Mais encore ici, ne nous y trompons pas: chaque étape graduelle vers la souveraineté extérieure du Canada est applaudie par les Canadiens-français, mais ils veulent bien conserver des anciens liens impériaux ce qui sauvegarde certains droits constitutionnels que leurs compatriotes peuvent mettre en péril.[21]

Dans la seconde phase de cette période, qui va du Statut de Westminster à la déclaration de guerre, il y a plusieurs reprises du provincialisme nationaliste des Canadiens-français, qui se trouvera sensibilisé, inquiet, et à certains moments, exarcerbé par la misère de la grande crise économique. Quand les nuages menaçants s'amoncellent sur le ciel européen à partir de 1935, les sympathies naturelles des Canadiens-français ne se porteront pas du même côté, comme on l'a vu lors des guerres éthiopienne et espagnole, que celui de leurs compatriotes. Ajoutons à cela une tradition renforcée d'anti-militarisme, ou plus exactement, d'anti-conscriptionnisme qu'a cultivée avec succès le parti libéral fédéral, au pouvoir à Ottawa pendant la plus grande partie de cette période, et l'on comprendra que le Canada français était aussi mal préparé qu'en 1914 à affronter la grande crise mondiale

[20] Brebner, *op. cit.*, p. 225.
[21] Par exemple, quand les Anglo-Canadiens favoriseront l'abolition des appels au Conseil Privé de Londres, comme instance judiciaire suprême, les Canadiens-français y verront une sauvegarde contre de possibles abus des instances judiciaires suprêmes du Canada.

de 1939. Comme un quart de siècle auparavant, le Canada menacera de se scinder en deux blocs rivaux.

Au sortir de la guerre, le Canada affirma nettement son indépendance des deux systèmes collectifs dont il faisait partie. D'abord à la Société des Nations en s'efforçant, à plusieurs reprises à partir du projet du Covenant, d'amoindrir la portée de l'article X[22] et y parvenant presque.[23] Un ministre canadien-français, Rodolphe Lemieux, disciple de Laurier, exprimait clairement la logique ultra simple du nouveau nationalisme canadien: "In military matters we are governed also by and from Ottawa, and not by and from London; and we do not want to be governed by and from Geneva." A diverses reprises, comme lors de l'incident de Chanak alors que le Canada refusa de participer automatiquement à une opération militaire aux côtés de l'Angleterre, comme lors de la signature du Halibut Treaty avec les Etats-Unis sans le paraphe de l'ambassadeur britannique, s'affirma le désir du Canada de conquérir sa majorité internationale. Le Canada sous Meighen et Mackenzie King pratiquait la politique de Laurier[24] et même celle de Bourassa.[25] Aux élections de 1925, King parlait le langage de Bourassa, non pas seulement dans le Québec, mais même en Ontario.[26]

A la conférence impériale de 1926, fut élaboré la définition désormais classique de cette chose qui n'avait pas eu d'équivalent historique:

[22] "The members of the League undertake to respect and preserve as against external aggression the territorial integrity and existing political independence of all Members of the League. In case of any such aggression or in case of any threat or danger of such aggression, the Council shall advise upon the means by which this obligation shall be fulfilled."

[23] A une voix près—celle de la Perse—, la dernière résolution canadienne faillit être votée, à l'unanimité. Mais comme la règle de l'unanimité prévalait, la résolution canadienne fut battue.

[24] "In the decade before the Great War the gentle but firm 'No!' of Laurier had defeated centralizing tendencies at London. In the post-War decade the ghost of Laurier was not less audible at Geneva." R. A. MacKay and E. B. Rogers, Canada Looks Abroad (Oxford University Press, 1938), p. 97.

[25] Après sa retraite, Borden "did much to formulate the new English-Canadian nationalism which he had helped to crystallize in the latter part of a career which had begun in the imperialist camp. In the end he had led in the realization of many of Bourassa's ideals for Canada. With the slow postwar development of English-Canadian nationalism, French Canadians were left less isolated politically, though the chasm between the races remained deep, thanks to the blood shed in Quebec in 1918," Mason Wade, The French Canadians 1760-1945 (New York, 1955), p. 775.

[26] "Just as we have gained self-government in domestic affairs, so in foreign affairs . . . we contend that they should be managed by our own people," cité par Wade, qui commente: "The thinking of both Bourassa and King on these matters had felt the common influence of Laurier upon his bright young men." Ibid., p. 807.

un "Dominion."[27]   Le Canada est maintenant à même d'exercer une politique étrangère à la fois autonome, mais solidaire—et d'une libre solidarité—avec ce qui allait devenir le Commonwealth.   Dans ce processus, il faut rappeler le rôle de précurseur de Bourassa, d'initiateur de Laurier, et d'actuel réalisateur de Lapointe, bras droit de King et successeur de Laurier comme fondé de pouvoir des Canadiens français au gouvernement fédéral.

Quand, quelques années plus tard, le Statut de Westminster (1931) vint consacrer officiellement et juridiquement l'évolution constitutionnelle de l'Empire depuis la fin de la guerre, d'anciennes voix nationalistes canadiennes-françaises se firent entendre au Parlement d'Ottawa, un Bourassa[28] un Lavergne,[29] qui parlèrent un langage à peu près identique à celui du premier ministre Bennett et d'Ernest Lapointe.

Le Statut de Westminster, qui passa à peu près inaperçu au Canada, était un évènement considérable.   L'Acte de l'Amérique du Nord britannique, qui créait la Confédération en 1867, donnait au Canada une réalité étatique; le Statut de Westminster lui accordait une plénitude internationale.   Les relations canado-impériales, dans le cadre plus souple et plus pragmatique du Commonwealth, allaient de moins en moins constituer un objet de dissension entre Canadiens des deux langues.   Mais, rançon d'une jeune indépendance extérieure, le Canada allait, comme malgré lui, prendre une conscience plus aigue de toutes les implications que comportait le voisinage des Etats-Unis. Il allait surtout être attiré dans le tourbillon des malaises internationaux croissants, qui préludaient à la seconde guerre mondiale.   Le premier ministre King disait en février 1936: "Our country is being drawn into international situations to a degree that I myself think is alarming."   La prudence, qui caractérisait encore plus qu'aujourd'-

[27] "They are autonomous Communities with the British Empire, equal in status, in no way subordinate to one another in any aspect of their domestic or external affairs, although united by a common allegiance to the crown, and freely associated as members of the British Commonwealth of Nations."

[28] ". . . je fais des voeux pour voir progresser non pas trop vite mais d'une façon constante le principe contenu dans cette loi et pour voir venir le jour où le Canada sera de nouveau à l'avant-garde, et non plus à l'arrière-garde, en ce qui concerne son affranchissement et son autonomie."   Michel Brunet, Guy Frégault, et Marcel Trudel, *Histoire du Canada par les Textes* (Montréal, 1952), p. 258.

[29] "Je suis un de ceux qui autrefois s'intitulaient "nationalistes," et je crois encore en la politique du "Canada d'abord," mais je suis également un de ceux qui reconnaissent leurs devoirs envers le roi et l'empire."   Et Lavergne de proposer que le Canada contribue avec d'autres Dominions à la liste civile du roi et de la famille royale!   *Ibid.*, p. 258.

hui la politique étrangère du Canada, incitait les hommes d'Etat canadiens moins à adopter des politiques efficaces que des attitudes variables et jamais trop définies pour ne pas risquer le fragile équilibre de l'unité nationale.

3.

Mais cet état de choses général ne signifie pas qu'on ne pouvait pas dégager un point de vue spécifiquement canadien-français sur telle ou telle question. Mais ce n'était pas toujours dans l'enceinte du Parlement, ou au sein des partis. Le Canadien français n'a jamais eu une foi très vive en la Société des Nations. Pour eux, la doctrine Monroe les protège bien plus efficacement surtout depuis que le président Roosevelt vient de déclarer, en 1936, que les Etats-Unis sont toujours prêts à défendre leur voisinage américain.

La raison essentielle de cette attitude, c'est qu'à l'encontre de l'Anglo-Canadien qui a une mère patrie en Europe, le Québecois, séparé de la France depuis un siècle et demi, est devenu un continental, un autochtone, comme l'Américain lui-même: rien ne l'intéresse nationalement en dehors de ses frontières. Enfin, autre attitude nord-américaine, il éprouve une certaine impatience devant ces nations d'Europe qui se ruinent en rivalités et en armements, lorsque lui, sans forteresse et sans armée, a su garder une paix séculaire avec son voisin.[30]

A l'époque des sanctions contre l'Italie, à peu près tous les journaux canadiens-français s'y opposèrent, suspectant la pureté d'intention des responsables de la décision, en particulier de l'Angleterre. Et Jean Bruchési, analysant l'attitude de ses compatriotes, disait en 1936: "Canada did of course vote for sanctions, but if the Province of Quebec had had to make the decision alone she certainly would not have adopted the line of conduct which was actually followed. With practical unanimity our French-Canadian press refused to dissimulate its sympathy with Italy by reason of sanctions."[31] Il en fut de même lors de la guerre civile d'Espagne. Les Canadiens français étaient,

---

[30] Lanctôt, *op. cit.*, pp. 277-278. On reconnaît là le symbole de l' "Ungarded frontier." Un député canadien-français, qui allait pendant de nombreuses années jouer le rôle d'un espèce de ministre suppléant aux affaires extérieures, Paul Martin, écrivait dans les années avant la guerre: "A purely European problem can best be settled by Europeans. If they cannot settle it, we cannot." Cité par MacKay et Rogers, *op. cit.*, p. 269.

[31] Cité par F. H. Soward, *Canada in World Affairs: The Pre-War Years* (Toronto, 1941), p. 24.

en grande majorité et manifestement, favorables aux forces du général Franco. Le corporatisme italien n'était pas loin d'être présenté comme modèle politique que le Portugal de Salazar toutefois réalisait avec encore plus de perfection. Même le national-socialisme allemand, malgré ses abus manifestes, n'avait pas que des vices. Mason Wade décrit assez justement cette atmosphère très spéciale où baignait le Canada français:

It was also difficult for the French Canadians, traditionally anti-imperialists, not to be skeptical of the new anti-imperialism of the English and the Americans as the Germans and Italians sought the empires which the other great powers had long enjoyed.

Preoccupied with its own economic and social troubles, French Canada had not shared the general Western development towards a belief in collective security; and as world conflagration came ever nearer, French Canada had lapsed more and more into isolationism. The old dream of a separate French Catholic State, a Laurentia, had never been more popular than in the immediate prewar period, thanks to the provincialist trend of Groulx' nationalism and to fears of the outside world.[32]

Pourtant, au moment de la déclaration de guerre, les Canadiens français étaient acquis au camp franco-britannique. L'alliance Molotov-Ribbentrop y était bien pour quelque chose. L'espèce de sympathie qu'ils portaient à l'Italie de Mussolini, en ce moment-là justement neutre, était bien compensée par l'antagonisme qu'ils portaient à la Russie, communiste et athée, coupable de la traîtrise suprême de s'allier à l'Allemagne hitlérienne. Le Canada n'allait déclarer la guerre aux forces de l'axe que le 10 septembre, marquant ainsi, par un acte distinct et plusieurs jours après Westminster, que le Canada n'était pas automatiquement en guerre du seul fait que la Grande-Bretagne l'était. Entre le 25 août et le 9 septembre, le gouvernement canadien louvoyait à travers les évènements qui se bousculaient à un rythme dramatique. Le cabinet King se refusait à prendre carrément position pour ou contre l'opposition conservatrice, favorable à la déclaration de guerre et à l'envoi d'une force expéditionnaire, ou pour ou contre un groupe de députés canadiens-français libéraux à tendance nationaliste qui prônaient l'abstention du Canada à toute guerre extérieure. Le premier ministre se rallia à une politique de "neutralité agressive," qui ménageait une retraite ou

[32] Wade, *op. cit.*, p. 916.

d'autres pas en avant, selon les fluctuations des deux opinions publiques canadienne-anglaise et canadienne-française.

Ce sera le numéro 2 du cabinet, Ernest Lapointe qui fera tomber les dernières résistances canadiennes-françaises dans une argumentation en deux points: 1—dans les circonstances actuelles, le Canada ne peut pas rester neutre; 2—notre participation devra exclure toute conscription. Sur le premier point, le Canada n'a pas le droit par sa neutralité d'encourager les ennemis de la France et de la Grande-Bretagne, et, d'ailleurs, "no government could stay in office if it refused to do what the large majority of Canadians wanted it to do" (i.e. l'envoi d'une force expéditionnaire). Quant au second point, Lapointe disait avec beaucoup d'insistance:

The whole province of Quebec—and I speak with all the responsibility and all the solemnity I can give to my words—will never agree to accept compulsory service or conscription outside Canada. I will go farther than that: When I say the whole province of Quebec I mean that I personally agree with them. I am authorized by my colleagues in the cabinet from the province of Quebec . . . to say that we will never agree to conscription and will never be members or supporters of a government that will try to enforce it. . . . May I add that if my friends and myself from Quebec were forced to leave the government, I question whether anyone would be able to take our place. . . . And those in Quebec who say that we will have conscription, in spite of what some of us are saying, are doing the work of disunity, the work of the foe, the work of the enemy. They weaken by their conduct and their words the authority of those who represent them in the government. . . . I will protect them against themselves. I believe the majority in my province trusts me; I have never deceived them, and I will not deceive them now. I have been told that my present stand means my political death. Well, at least it would not be a dishonourable end. But let me assure you . . . that if only I can keep my physical strength, fall I shall not, and my friends shall not fall, either.[33]

"L'opération sincérité" de M. Lapointe produisait ses effets à la chambre et dans l'opinion. Système de volontariat du service militaire, envoi d'un contingent militaire outre-mer, mais aussi participation modérée selon nos moyens:[34] telles furent les leitmotive de la

[33] Cité par Wade, pp. 920, 921.
[34] Un député canadien-français, J. H. Blanchette exprimait ainsi cette exigence qui allait prendre la forme d'un slogan: "I have reason to believe that I am expressing the opinion of the majority of electors in my province, in fact in all provinces, when I say that I am in favor of a reasonable and moderate cooperation, consistent with our interests and resources." Un autre député, Georges Héon prit le pouls, par

politique canadienne au début de la guerre. Les Canadiens français, dans leur ensemble, semblèrent accepter comme un pis-aller cette politique. Mais des groupes de provincialistes québecois s'exprimant dans leurs publications *Le Droit, Le Devoir,* et l'*Action nationale,* continuèrent à prêcher la non-intervention ou à annoncer les pires calamités, dont la conscription, du fait du principe de la participation canadienne.

La position du gouvernement fédéral se vit encore renforcée par l'élection provinciale du Québec, qui fut annoncée par M. Duplessis deux semaines après la déclaration de guerre. Durant la campagne, le parti de l'Union nationale plaça la lutte sur la question de la participation et la conscription. Son calcul fut déjoué. Ce fut une victoire éclatante du parti libéral de M. Godbout, aidé par les ministres canadiens-français du cabinet fédéral qui y avaient engagé tout le poids de leur prestige. Les Québecois s'en remettaient à leurs protecteurs fédéraux et à un chef provincial qui ne prenait aucune attitude extrémiste au sujet de la guerre et de l'unité nationale. Mais M. Godbout, pour mériter cette confiance, dut faire un serment aussi solennel que celui de M. Lapointe: "I pledge myself on my honour to quit my party and even to fight it if a single French Canadian, from now till the end of hostilities, is mobilized against his will under a Liberal regime, or even under a provisional regime in which our present ministers in the King cabinet participate."[35] Le Québec choisissait de ne pas se tenir à l'écart de la Confèdération[36] à une heure particulièrement grave.

Il n'y a pas que les généraux à faire la "guerre précédente": les hommes politiques et les peuples, surtout s'ils sont loin du théâtre des hostilités. Avec la *blitzkreig* et la défaite de la France, les Canadiens en ressentirent un vif choc.

---

un sondage, de ce que pensaient les électeurs de son comté: "15 per cent favored conscription to the last man and dollar, 20 per cent favored complete isolation, 65 per cent were 'for cooperation within our means and resources, preferably by the extension of credits, gifts of provisions and foodstuffs, and the manufacture of planes and munitions,' while there was 'a very strong and earnest sentiment against conscription of manpower' and opposition to an expeditionary force." Wade, *op. cit.,* pp. 919, 921-922.

[35] Cité par Wade, *op. cit.,* p. 930.

[36] Il y avait évidemment d'autres facteurs dans cette campagne, dont d'administration provinciale. "By its autocratic and extravagant regime which had doubled the debt of the province in three years, *l'Union Nationale* had alienated labor and offended the French-Canadian instinct for the way of moderation." *Ibid.,* p. 930.

From that moment the character of Canadian participation in the war was completely transformed—a change derived in part from the abrupt realization of the national danger, and also from the desire (particularly outside Quebec) to save the mother country and the ideals for which she stood. English-speaking Canada grasped more quickly the menace in-inherent in the situation, though the disaster to France soon brought conviction to French Canada also. In the latter instance, kinship with the motherland proved to be an unexpectedly poignant factor, and the French Canadians were themselves surprised at the depth and extent of their sympathies for the defeated and humiliated France.[37]

Le 24 juin, journée de Saint-Jean Baptiste, fête nationale des Canadiens-français, le premier ministre King leur disait qu'ils avaient "the duty of upholding the traditions of French culture and civilization and the French passion for liberty in the world."[38]

Peu après le Parlement d'Ottawa passait une loi qui était un acte de mobilisation générale à la restriction que les forces militaires du Canada ne seraient pas contraintes à servir en dehors du Canada ou de ses eaux territoriales. A cause de cette garantie, même Maxime Raymond, le plus influent des députés canadiens-français fédéraux à s'être prononcé contre la déclaration de guerre, vota pour la mesure. La législature du Québec eut bien à considérer une résolution de deux de ses députés ultra-nationalistes contre la loi de mobilisation; mais elle la repoussa par un vote de 56 à 13. Les autorités religieuses, le cardinal Villeneuve de Québec en tête, demandèrent à leur clergé d'expliquer la mesure à leurs fidèles et de les enjoindre à s'y soumettre. Le maire de Montréal, Camillien Houde, dans un geste d'une démagogie mal calculée, donna le conseil à ses administrés de ne pas se soumettre à la loi. Aussitôt interné pour cet acte de sédition, il fut désapprouvé par l'écrasante majorité de ses compatriotes.

Le recrutement volontaire des Canadiens français était depuis le début de la guerre beaucoup plus considérable qu'à l'autre guerre. Ce fut même un régiment canadien-français de Montréal qui fut le premier à compléter ses effectifs pour service outre-mer. L'acceptation relativement facile de la déclaration de la guerre et de la conscription aux seules fins de service sur le territoire canadien, jointe à de très honnêtes chiffres de recrutement pour service volontaire outre-mer, créèrent une certaine illusion chez beaucoup de Canadiens d'ex-

[37] Robert MacGregor Dawson, *Canada in World Affairs: Two Years of War, 1939-1941* (Toronto, 1943), p. 30.
[38] Cité par Wade, *op. cit.*, p. 932.

pression anglaise. En effet, les Canadiens français "marchaient" jusque là, mais c'était à la condition *sine qua non* qu'on n'établirait jamais la conscription pour service outre-mer.

On allait s'en rendre compte bientôt. A la fin de 1941, mourrait inopportunément Ernest Lapointe, le "rempart" des Canadiens-français à Ottawa. Après Pearl Harbor, les Etats-Unis allaient entrer en guerre avec la totalité de leurs ressources. La guerre prenait des proportions planétaires. Prévoyant des disettes d'effectifs, le gouvernement canadien tenta de se faire délier de ses promesses du début de la guerre. Il annonça un plébiscite national sur la question. Ce fut une étrange histoire. Le gouvernement fédéral faisait campagne pour le "oui" en argumentant qu'il ne s'agissait pas d'établir la conscription pour outre-mer immédiatement; mais seulement d'avoir le droit, le cas échéant, de considérer la question. La *Ligue pour la Défense du Canada*, d'où sortira plus tard le parti du *Bloc populaire Canadien* fit la campagne au Canada français. Le 27 avril 1942, le Québec vota "non" à une proportion de 72%, tandis que les autres provinces votèrent à 80% pour le "oui."[39] Les deux Canadas, comme en 1917, se retrouvaient face à face en radical désaccord sur une question décisive.

Mais ce ne sera qu'en novembre 1944 que la crise de la conscription éclatera véritablement. Dans l'intervalle, le Canada français aura vécu une existence agitée: sentiment d'insécurité, révolution socio-économique d'une industrialisation ultra-rapide, bouillonnement d'idées politiques diverses, y comprises, à la marge et de façon provisoire, celles du fascisme et de l'anti-sémitisme.[40] Avant même que les lourdes pertes des forces canadiennes en Europe n'aient causé une sérieuse crise des effectifs de notre armée, ce qui devait faire planer une fois de plus le spectre de la conscription, il y avait eu bien des attaques d'abord chuchotées, puis dites bien haut au sujet de l'"inégalité de sacrifice" entre soldats des deux groupes. Les éléments de la crise étaient aussi graves que ceux de 1917.

Mais beaucoup de choses étaient changées. Le ministère King se voyait accusé de manquer à ses solennelles promesses de 1939 dont le peuple canadien—sauf celui du Québec, au sujet duquel les promesses

[39] D'après une enquête Gallup en août 1942, 90% des Canadiens-français s'opposaient à la conscription tandis que 78% des Canadiens d'expression anglaise la favorisaient. *Ibid.*, p. 956.

[40] Cf. Wade, *op. cit.*, chap. xv dont une soixantaine de pages sont consacrées à la description de cette situation.

avaient été faites—l'avait délié quelques années plus tôt. Valait-il la peine de risquer une fois de plus une désunion nationale, peut-être celle-là définitive? Coup sur coup, King perdait deux ministres pour deux raisons contradictoires. Le cabinet était divisé. Les autorités militaires auraient considéré la possibilité d'un *putsch* si l'on ne trouvait pas les moyens de compenser pour les pertes subies au front.[41] La tension était extrême à travers tout le pays. Les cris de race avaient depuis quelque temps une âpreté qui rappelait la pire époque de 1917-1918.[42]

Au moment du vote décisif, le gouvernement King put s'assurer d'une confortable majorité de 143 à 70 mais 32 députés canadiens-français avaient voté contre le gouvernement. Après une analyse minutieuse de ces fameux débats, Mason Wade ne peut s'empêcher de conclure:

. . . Mackenzie King had won an overwhelming and incredible victory over Tory and nationalist opposition. These two poles of Canadian politics were not brought together in 1944 as they had been to defeat Laurier in 1911. . . . The support of the C.C.F. and Social Credit groups offset the defections of Quebec Liberals who broke with Mr. King and Mr. St.-Laurent. The result of the conscription debate was an index of the enormous development of Canadian national feeling in a third of a century. It was also a tribute to the consummate political skill of the man who had won a victory out of what had generally been regarded as certain defeat when the special session met on November 22.[43]

Le commun dénominateur de l'opinion et de la presse était exprimé par l'*Action Catholique* de Québec qui écrivait: ". . . we like a government that is conscriptionist 'in spite of itself' better than a conscriptionist government angry because compulsion has not been used sooner; we like a government which has reluctantly sacrificed Quebec better than a government which might have sought to sacrifice us still more, if not to be revenged upon us for our anti-conscriptionist stand. . . ."[44] On se souvient que l'imposition de la conscrip-

[41] Le moins qu'on puisse dire, c'est que ce point d'histoire n'a pas encore été éclairci.

[42] Pour les épisodes de cette crise extrêmement complexe nous nous contentons de renvoyer le lecteur à F. H. Soward, *Canada in World Affairs: From Normandy to Paris, 1944-1946* (Toronto, 1951), chap. II, pp. 31-50; et Wade, *op. cit.*, pp. 1022-1076.

[43] Wade, *op. cit.*, pp. 1068-69.

[44] Cité par Wade, *op. cit.*, p. 1073. Du point de vue d'un observateur étranger,

tion en 1917 n'avait guère amélioré la situation de notre armée canadienne. La même observation peut être faite au sujet de la crise de 1944. Le Canada aurait même pu, selon Mason Wade, faire l'économie d'une crise inutile.[45]

Et notre même auteur de conclure:

The 1944 conscription . . . provided another example of the periodic clashes of two very different Canadian mentalities. While the French Canadian frequently relieves his pent-up emotions, he does not allow emotion to sway him from following a reasonable course of action dictated by logic, although he may nurse bitterness long afterwards. On the other hand the English Canadian is much less given to emotional reactions, but when he does let common sense and reason yield to them, the outbreak is much more serious, though shortlived. The 1944 crisis was fortunately marked by less violence than the 1917-18 one, and hence its aftermath was much milder and shorter than was anticipated at the time. It is probable that the issue of conscription will never again split the peoples of Canada, who have twice learned the cost of trying to ride roughshod over the deepest emotions of French and English.[46]

Si l'avenir vérifie cette dernière assertion, il est plus que probable que ce soit pour une autre raison que celle que signale notre auteur: l'internationalisme nouveau des Canadiens-français l'aura emporté sur les progrès de l'unité nationale.

---

cette sagesse pratique n'avait été possible que parce que le gouvernement d'Ottawa avait su ne pas attaquer de front les convictions canadiennes-françaises. "Although most of French Canada was still shackled by an almost incurable isolationism and by a compulsive need to assert its separatism in many kinds of dissidence, it had been forced by external and domestic circumstances to look outward and to take some painful steps toward the acceptance of world citizenship. A cautious, sympathetic Government was prepared to shield it in the hope that it might shed enough of its defensive intransigeance to learn the satisfactions which could be derived from voluntary contribution to an all-Canadian cause. Canadian national unity after 1939 was largely a formal unity, for it involved the difficult task of persuading the English-speaking majority to exercise their imaginations and their tolerance instead of their prejudices in thought, word, and action where French Canada was concerned. No one on either side expected miracles, but the thoughtful knew that every minute gain in conscious collaboration was worth far more than years of lip service toward making Canada more of a nation." Brebner, *op. cit.*, p. 319.

[45] "The reinforcement crisis of 1944 was in great measure an artificial one brought on by the unscrupulous efforts of a party long in opposition to win power at any cost. The stake was not military victory in Europe, which was already assured, or the defense of Canada's reputation and honor, which had already been upheld beyond imputation, but control of Canada in a postwar world full of dangers for the conservative-minded." Wade, *op. cit.*, pp. 1075-1076.

[46] *Ibid.*, p. 1076.

4.

Dans son histoire, l'indéfectible—parce qu'instinctive—résolution de rester soi-même a toujours animé les Canadiens français. Il est arrivé que cela ait coïncidé avec l'intérêt du Canada à venir ou existant; en 1775, 1812, 1849, 1867. Il est arrivé que cela ait semblé contredire l'unité nationale à faire, ou le degré d'unité réalisée: en 1899, 1911, 1917, 1942, 1944. Dans les premiers cas, le monde extérieur auquel on disait "non" était les Etats-Unis. Dans les seconds, c'était un monde extérieur, mal défini, menaçant, et d'autant plus inquiétant qu'il fallait intervenir principalement à cause de notre appartenance à la grande famille britannique. En ces derniers cas, le refus était double: à l'internationalisme et au britannisme. Dans les premiers cas, le refus était simple: à l'américanisme, mais il comportait acceptation du britannisme, au moins de ses formes politiques institutionnelles. Quand il y avait refus du britannisme, c'était contre l'autorité britannique qui se faisait sentir le plus lourdement, soit de Londres, soit d'Ottawa.

Cette volonté de durer tout en restant différent a été baptisé "nationalisme." Nous préférions dire plutôt "provincialisme," parce que, selon nous, un "nationalisme" aux 19ᵉ et 20ᵉ siècles, tend, par sa nature à être d'*émancipation* et, à une phase ultérieure, de *domination*.[47] Il ne peut se contenter d'être un simple nationalisme culturel. Il y eut presque toujours de petits groupes qui ont prôné un nationalisme d'*émancipation*, un "séparatisme" du Canada-français. Mais ce furent toujours et ce sont encore des groupes à très maigres clientèles sans influence aucune sur les évènements. Mais le "provincialisme" canadien-français est une réalité historique d'une toute autre importance: il s'agissait d'avoir une "province" française bien à soi en cette Amérique du Nord, ce qui s'accomplit en deux temps en 1791 et en 1867. A partir de là, la vie collective canadienne-français prenait les caractères du *provincialisme*, i.e. repli sur soi, au nom de valeurs estimées transcendantes,[48] le moins de perméabilité aux influences extérieures,[49] cohésion et homogénéité de l'ensemble pour

---

[47] Il est de plus en plus frappant de constater qu'un parti nationaliste n'ait pu se maintenir au Canada. Au contraire, un parti dont le provincialisme est aussi accentué que celui de l'Union nationale se maintient au pouvoir depuis 16 ans, après avoir été le gouvernement de la Province de Québec de 1936 à 1939.

[48] Catholicisme et culture française.

[49] Et l'extérieur commençant aussi bien à l'ouest de la rivière Ottawa qu'au sud du 45ᵉ parallèle.

pouvoir, à l'occasion, mieux se défendre, etc. Ce *provincialisme* se rattachait à un cadre plus vaste: un état bi-ethnique où la province française acceptait d'être, à perpétuité, minoritaire. Ceux qui, dans la politique ou l'administration fédérale, accomplissaient des rôles d'importance au niveau de l'état canadien se défendaient mal de ne pas agir en "fondés de pouvoir" ou en "ministres plénipotentiaires" de la province française, puisqu'en outre de leur psychologie profonde qui ne se démentait pas, ils savaient qu'ils seraient jugés ultimement par leur fidélité française. Enfin le Canadien français se cantonnait principalement dans une des deux grandes provinces centrales. Il y a au Canada juridiquement 10 provinces ou "Etats provinciaux," 4 ou 5 régions géographico-économiques naturelles, mais il y a, ethniquement, deux *provinces:* celle qui parle français et celle qui parle anglais.

Sans moyens d'accès direct à l'internationalisme qui se présentait presqu'exclusivement sous les couleurs de l'empire britannique, auto-fermé systématiquement à la sollicitation américaine estimée encore plus périlleuse pour la communauté de destin, toujours conscient du danger d'être absorbé par un grand tout canadien, le nationalisme canadien-français trouvait son point d'insertion politique par l'affirmation continue d'un *provincialisme* très accusé à l'intérieur de la vaste réalité canadienne. L'histoire canadienne jusqu'à 1945 ne confirmerait que la première partie de notre hypothèse: le fait du provincialisme. En fait, l'hypothèse complète (passage du provincialisme à l'internationalisme) ne prendrait corps qu'après, vers 1950, sans qu'on ne puisse dire avec certitude si la guerre de Corée est une cause ou une simple coïncidence du processus d'éclatement de ce provincialisme. Mais il importe assez peu de déterminer avec précision le point de repère. Ce qui importe, c'est de voir le curieux processus par où les Canadiens-français dans la mesure où ils cessent d'être "provinciaux," ne semblent pas devenir plus "pan-canadiens," mais bien, plus cosmopolites, "internationalistes" d'esprit et d'attitude. C'est là la nouveauté, l'intérêt de la situation nouvelle. En matière de politique officielle, il en est actuellement comme dans la période de l'entre-deux guerres: les Canadiens français ne peuvent aller plus loin que la politique canadienne elle-même. Leur influence est principalement négative, de freinage et se fait sentir à l'intérieur du parti[50]

[50] Depuis 1896, ce parti est principalement le parti libéral; l'influence dans et par le parti conservateur n'a jamais été forte ni continue. A l'heure actuelle, elle est sous M. Diefenbaker à son plus bas niveau depuis 60 ans, sauf pendant la décennie de 1911 à 1921.

au pouvoir. Mais les processus dont nous faisons état sont plus diffus et incomparablement plus vastes que les attitudes ou les prises de position de politiciens canadiens-français en regard des politiques officielles du gouvernement canadien.

Quand le Canadien français est confronté par les réalités internationales les plus pressantes: les guerres mondiales, celle de Corée, l'expédition de Suez, il transpose comme tout naturellement les schèmes politiques ultra-simples ("nous" et "les autres") par lesquels il définit sa position de provincial minoritaire dans un continent à prépondérance anglo-saxonne. Son attitude en chaque cas est conditionnée par l'extension qu'il peut donner au "nous" et par la détermination exacte du point où commencent "les autres."

Le "canadianisme"[51] a fait des progrès énormes depuis 1945. Plus d'un observateur l'a noté. Mais ce "nous" dit par un Canadien français, quand il cesse de vouloir dire "nous Québecois," ou "nous Canadiens français," dit tout autant volontiers "nous Nord-américains," "nous pays atlantiques," "nous du monde libre," etc. que "nous citoyens canadiens" ou que "nous Etat canadien." Ce phénomène n'est curieux qu'en apparence. On ne sent plus "nous" avec un étranger lointain qu'on ne connaît pas mais qui est un partenaire inévitable qu'avec un concitoyen qu'on a considéré séculairement comme ennemi ou, tout au moins, comme un rival. Le canadianisme a marqué des points depuis une douzaine d'années; mais nous voudrions proposer que l'internationalisme à l'âge de la fusée intercontinentale et de la Bombe H,[52] en a marqué de plus rapides encore dans la psychologie politique du Canadien-français. L'élargissement du provincialisme canadien n'attend plus la médiation d'un canadianisme satisfaisant[53] pour passer au stade de l'internationalisme pratique.

[51] Formule commode pour parler du nationalisme pan-canadien et de la place qu'y tient le provincialisme canadien-français. Ou mieux: de leur complémentarité nécessaire, de plus en plus clairement ressentie, et, conséquemment de leur attraction réciproque qui *commence timidement* à se faire sentir.

[52] Le Canada français découvre depuis peu qu'il est situé sur la ligne droite qui relie Washington à Moscou.

[53] Il est assez curieux de constater que lorsqu'ils défendaient âprement leur provincialisme, les Canadiens-français arboraient souvent les couleurs d'un canadianisme d'anticipation. Maintenant que ce canadianisme tend à s'inscrire de plus en plus dans la réalité canadienne, ils ne semblent pas être pressés de profiter des nouvelles chances qui leur sont offertes. En fait, ils ne les voient guère.

Ce qui n'interdit pas des accomodements à la John C. Calhoun! L'histoire des partis en offrirait quelques exemples: en 1945, les Canadiens-français continuèrent, moins d'un an après la "trahison" de l'imposition de la conscription, à faire la bonne fortune du parti libéral fortement majoritaire, et ce jusqu'en 1957; de même, en 1958, ils ne manquèrent pas la nouvelle vague conservatrice qui déferla sur tout le

Le nationalisme pan-canadien s'affirme de plus en plus sur le plan international. Il tend même à prendre l'allure d'un anti-américanisme, non pas certes virulent mais systématique. C'est dû à l'énorme attraction économique et militaire qu'exerce les Etats-Unis sur le Canada. Brebner les a déjà comparés à des "jumeaux siamois." Il faudrait peut-être ajouter que l'un des jumeaux a démesurément grandi, qu'il a un appétit gigantesque et qu'il affiche de forts instincts d'indépendance et de puissance, tandis que l'autre voudrait bien continuer de mener sa vie de petit garçon sage sans grande ambition.[54]

Dans cet anti-américanisme de beaucoup de Canadiens anglophones, il y a le sentiment d'une très vive insécurité. Ils se sentent trop peu de distance psychologique et culturelle d'avec les Américains. Ce n'est pas seulement une question de langue, mais la langue ne constituant pas une barrière, mais bien un utile canal d'influences, ces dernières jouent à fond. Au Canada français l'anglais reste toujours appris, une langue seconde, quelque chose d'artificiel, de plaqué. L'*American Way of Life* a enlevé depuis longtemps l'*Unguarded Frontier* de la culture anglo-canadienne. Un fonds commun d'anglosaxonnisme, transformé par le climat nord américain, rendait l'involontaire conquête naturelle et facile. Aussi l'Anglo-canadien, se sentant trop identique à l'Américain, n'a guère d'autre ressource, quant à lui, que de réaffirmer son "canadianisme." Mais à l'examen,[55] il s'aperçoit que le canadianisme consiste en des différences d'avec l'américanisme ("être canadien, c'est n'être pas américain") et il est amené tout naturellement, pour établir ce contraste, à exagérer parfois les sources britanniques de sa culture. Comme le disait l'humoriste canadien, Stephen Leacock: "Le Canadien est un homme qui passe la moitié de sa vie à montrer aux Américains qu'il n'est pas un Anglais et l'autre moitié à montrer aux Anglais qu'il n'est pas un Américain, ce qui ne lui laisse plus de temps pour être canadien."[56]

---

pays et se rallièrent massivement au parti avec lequel ils avaient été en relations tendues depuis plus d'un demi-siècle.

[54] Le Seminar de Duke University de 1958 portait précisément sur "The American Economic Impact on Canada." Cette année les articles des Professeurs Bladen et MacInnis évoquent le fait de la grande dépendance du Canada par rapport aux Etats-Unis dans la conduite de sa politique étrangère.

[55] "Dans cette poursuite après soi-même, dans cette course à l'auto-découverte, le Canada rencontre à chaque virage la grande ombre des U.S.A." Hans J. Morgenthau, "Les Relations canado-américaines," *Rapport de la cinquième Conférence annuelle de l'Institut canadien des Affaires publiques*, (Sainte-Agathe, P. Q., Canada, 1959) p. 12.

[56] Citation de mémoire.

Nous semblons nous éloigner de notre sujet. Pas tant que cela. Les réflexes primaires tout autant que les attitudes raisonnées en politique étrangère découlent des faits culturels les plus constants et les plus profonds. Prenons un exemple concret: la collaboration militaire entre les deux pays nord-américains. Depuis l'accord d'Ogdensburg de 1940 jusqu'aux accords récents de NORAD en passant par l'établissement des réseaux transcontinentaux de radar, les Anglo-Canadiens voient rétrécir la zone de leur libre disposition en matière de défense, et, de façon générale, dans toute leur politique étrangère. En cette même université, le Professeur Underhill pouvait dire il y a quelques années: "They [the Canadians] are aware that they spent one hundred years, from 1839 to 1939, in achieving their independence from Great Britain; and they wonder whether they will have to spend the hundred years from the Ogdensburg agreement of 1940 in maintaining their independence against the United States. Some of them fear that the United States is already building up an empire over them in a fit of absence of mind."[57] Ils sont plus que jamais méfiants des entreprises américaines en matière économique ou militaire. Car très souvent, elles les heurtent. Il s'ensuit une atmosphère de récriminations presque perpétuelles. Les Canadiens ne s'en privent pas d'autant que les Américains ont autant besoin du Canada que vice-versa.[58]

Le Canadien français, lui, n'est pas plus foncièrement inquiet depuis que la puissance américaine est devenue déterminante dans l'équilibre du monde. Sur lui, comme groupe, l'influence américaine ne le presse pas plus proportionnellement que par le passé. Tandis que l'anti-américanisme de l'Anglo-canadien s'est constitué des pressions diverses et sans cesse croissantes, qui provenaient de la coexistence inégale avec les Etats-Unis,—d'autant plus ressenties que se relâchaient dans le même temps les liens d'avec Londres—, le Canadien français, lui, a depuis toujours, et de tous côtés, été soumis à des pressions diverses. Il a l'habitude de l'inégalité pour ne pas dire de l'"infériorité." La situation d'Etat protégé qui semble être son destin, pour un temps indéfini encore, ne l'humilie pas. On s'habitue au protectorat. Culturellement, le Canadien-français est bien plus

---

[57] Underhill, *op. cit.*, pp. 97-98.

[58] "Canadians, no matter how we behave, are not expendable. The United States must defend us to the last. If Canada is ever abandoned to the enemy, it will be on the day before Chicago and Detroit are abandoned. Hence the remarkable freedom and frequency with which our Secretary of State for External Affairs delivers public lectures to the State Department." *Ibid.*, pp. 71-72.

protégé que son concitoyen de langue anglaise de la contagion de l'américanisme—même si, en surface, et même un peu plus en profondeur, il vit à l'américaine.[59]   La conséquence en est que l'Anglo-canadien trouve moins en sa substance profonde ce qui donne au Canada sa configuration propre que dans ce qu'apporte le fait de l'existence de Franco-canadiens.   Certains vont même jusqu'à dire que l'existence du Canada-français est le seul signe de distinction du Canada des Etats-Unis.

L'attraction réciproque de ce nationalisme canadien-anglais et de ce provincialisme québecois peut être très prometteur pour l'unité nationale et la constitution d'un nationalisme pan-canadien.   Mais nous n'en sommes pas là.   Aux préjugés anciens succèdent les abîmes d'ignorance mutuelle.   Et les dernières réticences risquent de venir du côté canadien-français.   Le Canada français ne refuse pas la réalité Canada; il en a à peine conscience.   Et dans la mesure où il en prend conscience, un certain vertige le prend: celui d'être dissous ou digéré dans un tout qui sera de moins en moins à sa mesure démographique. Tandis que les exigences de la vie internationale ne comportent pas le même risque: l'internationalisme se déroule à l'enseigne de la solidarité et de la coopération et l'unité représentative, l'agent de négociation, est le Dominion du Canada.   Dans l'ensemble des complexes (Canada-Etats-Unis, Communauté Atlantique, Commonwealth, O.N.U.) où se déroulent les plus importantes des relations internationales du Canada, le Canada français ne se sent pas menacé, n'étant même pas identifié.   Il y a là une condition négative utile à un sain internationalisme, à une ouverture sur le monde.

Laquelle de ces aspirations (vers un canadianisme ou vers un internationalisme) que subit le provincialisme canadien-français l'emportera ultimement?   Evidemment, on n'en sait rien.   Notons d'abord qu'elles ne sont pas contradictoires, mais qu'elles seraient plutôt complémentaires: un sain nationalisme, relativement achevé, pouvant prédisposer à un internationalisme mesuré et efficace.   Notre hypothèse ne nous permet que de saisir que les Canadiens-français sont au début d'un processus ambivalent où l'attraction de l'internationalisme les solliciterait, davantage et à un rythme plus rapide, que celui du canadianisme.   Les Canadiens anglais auraient passé selon un ordre logique du colonialisme au canadianisme.   Les Cana-

[59] Cela serait un beau sujet que nous ne pouvons toucher.   Car, "c'est une autre histoire."

diens français seraient en train de passer du provincialisme à l'internationalisme, sans la médiation logique du canadianisme.

On le verrait à plusieurs signes: les intellectuels et les milieux étudiants définissent leurs préoccupations majeures selon des dimensions humaines, universelles d'intention. A la trilogie de la génération précédente: "nationalisme, patriotisme, ordre," ils ont substitué la trilogie: "démocratie, civisme, liberté." Leurs compagnes en matière d'éducation se font au nom du droit fondamental de l'homme à l'instruction et non pas pour la défense de la culture canadienne-française, envisagée comme résultat désirable et non pas comme objectif à atteindre. Il y a plus: il faut parler d'un mépris presque systématique—et qui, décidément, va trop loin—du nationalisme enveloppant dans une commune désapprobation ceux qui, au nom de cette idée, mènent des combats d'arrière-garde.[60] On les considère comme des anachronismes vivants.[61]

L'éclatement du provincialisme de naguère serait, théoriquement, aussi favorable à l'éclosion d'un sain et nécessaire canadianisme qu'à une ouverture plus large vers l'internationalisme. Il n'est pas dit que, dans ce processus ambivalent, ce ne soit le canadianisme qui marque des progrès dans la phase prochaine. Les Canadiens français, même enveloppés dans leur provincialisme, ont toujours été plus canadiens que leurs compatriotes de langue anglaise. Le canadianisme de ceux-ci n'a guère d'autre expression que celle de contrastes, parfois assez tenus, avec l'américanisme et le britannisme. Au niveau des associations nationales et des fédérations d'associations, la collaboration entre Canadiens des deux langues s'est considérablement accrue,

[60] On objectera que des petits groupes de jeunes, habituellement réunis autour d'une revue, se sont multipliés ces dernières années. S'intitulant plus farouchement encore "de droite" que "nationalistes," ces groupes n'ont guère d'audience notable, ni du point de vue qualitatif, ni quantitatif. C'est d'ailleurs un phénomène "cyclique" de l'histoire des idées politiques au Canada français que la résurgence de ces petites chapelles.

[61] Le projet de célébration du bi-centenaire de la bataille des Plaines d'Abraham de 1759 (qui scellait le sort de la Nouvelle-France) a permis encore récemment l'expression de certaines vieilles idiosyncrasies sur la mentalité de "vaincus." Un homme qui, pendant toute sa carrière, s'est identifié à ce qu'il y avait de vivant dans le nationalisme canadien-français, André Laurendeau, écrivait à ce sujet: ". . . on aurait tort de vouloir tirer une politique d'une nostalgie . . . je me demande pourquoi nous nous installerions dans une posture de vaincus. Et continuer, après deux siècles, de regarder une défaite militaire comme une tache et un déshonneur, il me semble que c'est un peu cela. . . . Ou bien c'est regarder les perspectives d'avant 1759 comme faciles à reprendre et à réaliser dans l'avenir. . . . Mais alors, on détourne son peuple des tâches possibles au profit d'une chimère: celle de l'indépendance politique totale du Canada français." *Le Devoir*, 25 juin 1959, p. 4.

en étendue, en fréquence et en sérieux, depuis une dizaine d'années. Mais c'est là le fait des dirigeants supérieurs des dites associations; et il est moins que prouvé que le "rank and file" soit au même degré d'évolution.

Si un canadianisme adulte et vivace doit un jour prendre forme, il devra s'exprimer en un sur-nationalisme ou en un pluralisme de nationalismes.[62] Encore une fois, plus me frappe, à l'heure actuelle, l'aspiration vers un internationalisme, bien sûr vaporeux et d'essence plutôt négative, qui semble suffisant toutefois pour faire craquer les cadres provincialistes traditionnels des Canadiens français, que leur contribution positive à un canadianisme encore très hypothétique.

Encore une fois, je ne fais qu'établir le caractère plausible d'une hypothèse qu'il est, de toute façon, trop tôt de vérifier dans un sens ou l'autre. Je n'ignore pas que l'élite intellectuelle du Canada-fran-çais ne porte qu'un intérêt très, très relatif aux affaires internationales, que dans nos universités l'étude des relations internationales (et de la science politique) en est encore à ses premiers balbutiements. Mais je vois, d'autre part, que nos journaux sont en train d'améliorer nettement leurs pages internationales,[63] que notre télévision française a trouvé un auditoire massif et infiniment curieux à un programme de commentaires internationaux.[64] Nos étudiants universitaires montrent une curiosité active vraiment étonnante au sujet des problèmes que

[62] Dont le trait commun essentiel sera que ces nationalismes devront être dénués de ce qu'un collègue de l'auteur, Maurice Tremblay, appelle "de charges affectives" de part et d'autre. Gérard Filion écrivait récemment: "200 ans de vie commune, c'est bien peu pour bâtir un pays; il en a fallu quatre ou cinq fois plus pour faire la Suisse. Cessons de nous faire des compliments et d'essayer de nous faire accroire que nous nous aimons; ce n'est pas vrai. Mais nous représentons de part et d'autre assez de qualités solides pour faire un mariage de raison. C'est sans doute moins chaud, mais ça peut être plus durable," Le Devoir, 20 juin 1959, p. 4. A quelques jours d'intervalle, un autre directeur d'un journal influent, Jean-Louis Gagnon, écrivait aussi: "On a dit de la Chine ancienne qu'elle avait été moins une nation qu'une civilisation. N'est-ce pas un peu le sort qui nous échoit?" La Presse, 23 juin 1959.

[63] Le journal qui présente les meilleures chroniques internationales au Canada est le journal canadien-français, dit "nationaliste," Le Devoir. Et des journaux à fort tirage comme La Presse de Montréal et le Soleil de Québec font depuis peu un effort plus que louable dans le sens indiqué.

[64] Point de Mire, animé par René Lévesque. La nouvelle de la suspension de cette émission a soulevé de très vives et nombreuses protestations de la part des téléspectateurs. Ce programme, fort bien fait, était dans la catégorie des émissions dites "sérieuses" qui ne font pas de concessions de facilité. Le talent hors pair de l'animateur n'aurait pu utilement s'employer sans une "faim," sans doute peu com-mune chez un aussi grand nombre de téléspectateurs, de connaître l'évolution de la situation internationale.

pose le sous-développement des régions déshéritées du globe. L'expérience personnelle de l'auteur comme conférencier devant des groupes fort divers ou comme participant à des émissions de radio-télévision confirme un état d'extraordinaire réceptivité pour la compréhension des questions internationales. D'autre part, c'est devenu presque un snobisme pour le jeune canadien-français "brillant" de se diriger vers la carrière diplomatique; le ministère des Affaires extérieures est probablement le seul où les Canadiens-français détiennent, à tous les niveaux, une influence proportionnelle à leur nombre. M. Saint-Laurent fut notre premier ministre des Affaires étrangères; plus que quiconque il fut responsable de l'élaboration de la politique étrangère canadienne dans l'après-guerre et on sait le rôle majeur qu'il tint dans la phase préliminaire de l'OTAN. De jeunes députés canadiens-français, MM. Lesage et Cardin, sont devenus assistants-parlementaires aux affaires extérieures. Il y a un assentiment de base des Canadiens-français sur les grandes politiques de l'OTAN, de la défense conjointe avec les Etats-Unis, du Commonwealth, du Plan de Colombo, de l'O.N.U. Lorsqu'il s'est agi de fournir des soldats canadiens aux forces internationales, lors des conflits de Corée et de Suez, le réflexe instinctif de l'anti-militarisme de naguère n'a pas joué. C'est là une conquête de l'internationalisme, non du canadianisme.

Pouvons-nous aller aussi loin que de dire que le service militaire obligatoire ne constituerait plus une pierre d'achoppement comme par le passé? Nous serions tentés de répondre: "oui." Et pour plusieurs raisons: 1—l'épouvantail de la guerre impériale n'existe plus; 2—l'armée s'est canadianisée et a même fait quelques efforts de bilinguisme; 3—le Canadien-français s'est habitué à considérer la vie militaire comme carrière, et il ne voit plus en elle une école de perdition morale ou une antichambre de "boucherie"; 4—l' "éventuel ennemi" n'éveille plus aucune sympathie pour les valeurs qu'il incarne comme c'était le cas pour, sinon l'Allemagne hitlérienne, du moins le fascisme de Mussolini et autres dictatures latines comme l'Espagne et le Portugal. Où l'on voit que l'anticonscriptionnisme systématique de naguère recouvrait beaucoup moins un anti-militarisme ou même un anti-bellicisme qu'un anti-impérialisme (en autant que celui-ci était ou apparaissait être négateur de canadianisme).

5.

Depuis 1945, il est assez difficile de dire très exactement ce qui est changé par rapport aux années de guerre dans la psychologie canadienne-française. Il faudrait—ce qu'à Dieu ne plaise!—des crises ou des chocs comparables à ceux de 1944 ou 1917. Ce dont on peut faire état, ce sont des séries d'indices, qui n'existaient pas dans les périodes qui précédaient les crises antérieures; c'est une ambiance ou un climat, beaucoup plus larges, pour ne pas dire plus généraux, qui tend à faire se dilater le provincialisme de naguère. Mais contrairement à une opinion reçue sur le sujet, je dirais que ce provincialisme en s'ouvrant, est aspiré par un internationalisme plus encore que par un canadianisme, qui n'est encore trop, du reste, qu'une forme de régionalisme culturel d'essence principalement négative. Cette aspiration est d'ailleurs inscrit dans la nature des choses: voisinage immédiat des mondes américain et soviétique; imprégnation, mais non absorption, par l'américanisme; refus et crainte non morbide du soviétisme; adaptation des valeurs et institutions politiques britanniques; liens intellectuels profonds, qui n'ont jamais été rompus, quoiqu'ayant toujours manqué de vivacité, avec la plus universelle des cultures nationales: la française:[65] c'est là un lourd héritage.[66]

Je voulais simplement appuyer l'idée principale qui est: *de même que les nécessités de l'internationalisme d'aujourd'hui ont fait éclater l'esprit colonial de naguère de beaucoup d'Anglo-canadiens, ces mêmes nécessités sont en train d'élargir, et, éventuellement, de féconder en internationalisme le provincialisme du Canada français.* Qu'il sorte, comme sous-produit de ce double processus, un canadianisme viable, cela ne peut être qu'un enrichissement, ou un complément, pour l'américanisme lui-même.

[65] L'auteur voudrait dire au lecteur qu'il est pleinement conscient que le langage qu'il faut pour exprimer ces choses peut sembler quelque peu ampoulé. Un extraordinaire carrefour d'influences ne prédispose pas à devenir le centre du monde!

[66] Il y aurait lieu d'ajouter aussi le fait du catholicisme de l'écrasante majorité des Canadiens-français. L'oecuménisme de la religion catholique—"catholique" voulant dire, étymologiquement, "universel"—incline-t-il à une forme d'universalisme politique, qui serait ce qu'on nous avons appelé "internationalisme"? Nous ne saurions dire: mais nous accepterions, par hypothèse, une correspondance d'une certaine nature entre les modes de perception des valeurs religieuses et des valeurs politiques. Il y aurait, par exemple, à étudier la signification politico-religieuse du fait que le Canada français est un des peuple les plus missionnaires du monde.

7

Economic Aspects of Foreign Policy

Vincent W. Bladen

When I first agreed to address this Seminar I thought that I would discuss some of the specific economic issues in Canadian relations with other countries, and in particular with the United States. I might have said something about current worries over the heavy capital imports from the United States: deploring the behavior of politicians in whipping up ill-feeling, recognizing the enormous value of these imports in permitting rapid expansion with less inflation, and suggesting the wisdom of arrangements by which Canadians could share in the equity of American subsidiaries in Canada.[1] I might have discussed the difficulties of marketing Canadian wheat in a world where many countries would not buy however cheap and others sell, or give away, regardless of cost.[2] I might have talked about the problem of oil[3] and minerals subject to embargoes or quantitative restrictions, and of commodities without number subject to the uncertainties of tariff administration.[4] At a time when the great co-operative venture, the Seaway, has just been opened, I might be writing about the problems of arranging international co-operation in the Columbia water system. Finally, I might have examined the exasperating experiments in extraterritorial application of the anti-trust laws.[5] But I propose to do none of these things: first, because

[1] See Royal Commission on Canada's Economic Prospects, *Preliminary Report* (Ottawa, 1956), chap. xiv, and *Final Report* (Ottawa, 1957), chap. xviii.

[2] See W. E. Hamilton and W. M. Drummond, *Wheat Surpluses and Their Impact on Canada-United States Relations* (Canadian-American Committee, 1959).

[3] John Davis, *Oil and Canada-United States Relations* (Canadian-American Committee, 1959).

[4] See G. A. Elliott, *Tariff Procedures and Trade Barriers* (Toronto, 1955).

[5] The Canadian Minister of Justice, the Honorable E. D. Fulton, discussed this problem in an address to the Anti-trust section of the New York State Bar Association, in New York, January 28, 1959. He referred in particular to the complaint filed November 24, 1958, against General Electric, Westinghouse, and N. V. Philips.

I do not know enough about any of them and I have not had time to do the necessary work to permit intelligent discussion; but, second and more important, because there are some general considerations, applicable to the foreign policy of the United States as well as of Canada, and indeed of all the NATO countries, which should be discussed. As an economic theorist and a close student of the literature of "liberal" economics I think I can make a more useful contribution by raising some issues of principle.

In the last year or so there has been a good deal of criticism in Canada of some of the economic policies and actions of the United States. I have said that I do not propose to discuss these, but I do want to begin with a reference not to the issues but to the fact of angry and unrestrained comment. Indeed it is this tone of Canadian public discussion that suggested the line of argument on which I have embarked. Canadians should remember that the world is listening in. In the Communist world we, of the Western Alliance, are designated as "imperialist" and "expansionist." Many other countries, some uncommitted, others committed in some degree to the Western Alliance, believe, suspect, or fear that this designation is deserved. Canadians in these countries are in the best position to counteract the fears and suspicions aroused by the might of the United States. But we cannot tell the Pakistani that Americans can be trusted and fill Canadian papers with angry complaints about oil embargoes. The world is now too small for that. I do not mean that we cannot discuss these serious issues in public. We must. But I do urge that we in Canada improve the tone of that discussion: it may not be misconstrued in the United States but a less friendly world is listening in, and it may be seriously misconstrued to the damage not just of the

Operating through Canadian subsidiaries (mostly Canadian companies) they were alleged to be engaged in an unlawful conspiracy in restraint of foreign trade. Yet the Canadian patent pool which was held to violate the U.S. anti-trust laws was not considered to violate the Canadian combines legislation. Another example is the I.C.I.-Dupont case which forced the reorganization of a Canadian company. Such was the extraordinarily extraterritorial effect of this decree that an application had to be made to a U.S. court so as to permit one Canadian company to sell a product made in Canada to another Canadian company for resale and distribution in Canada without penalty to directors in the U.S. It is not a healthy state when the Province of Ontario has to pass legislation making it an offense for Ontario companies to take documents out of the country, and when a court in the United States affirms its power to grant discovery from foreign files *despite prohibition of foreign laws*. Such "imperialism" with a view to breaking monopoly may be very different from monopolistic imperialism; but it is not consistent with national aspirations or with good international relations.

United States but of the Western Alliance as a whole. Irresponsible comment may prove dreadfully costly. I shall later have something to say about irresponsible action to which this irresponsible comment is a response.

I.

I want first to examine the designation "imperialist." I take it that the term implies that we seek political domination, that the motivation of such political domination is economic, and that the economic result is exploitation of the "colonial" countries mainly in the interest of the *bourgeoisie* of the "imperialist" countries, though the gains may be shared with the "aristocracy of labor" with a view to averting proletarian revolt. Along with this goes a belief that "imperialism" being the "highest form of capitalism" is an inevitable stage in its development so that political ideals of mutuality and peace are "utopian"; capitalism, or rather "monopoly capitalism," involves inevitable conflict of "imperialist" nations over the "colonial" markets, in which conflicts the "capitalists" will enlist the political authority of their respective countries. Whether the basis for this be Hobson's theory of underconsumption; or Lenin's division of markets to avoid competition, investment of capital abroad to postpone the decline in the rate of profit, and struggle for the source of supply of crucial raw materials; the fundamental argument is that national power is sought and used for the economic advantage of the powerful, and that power is a source of plenty, for the "rentiers" and possibly for the favored, "bourgeoisified" members of the proletariat. In saying all this I assume that Lenin's pamphlet on imperialism,[6] which owed so much to Hobson's earlier study,[7] is influential in Communist circles. If it is not I would argue the necessity for understanding what is meant currently by our designation as "imperialist." We must try to understand how we appear to our enemies.

If we look back over our history, of action and thought, we find a precapitalist period of "imperialism" when power seemed at times to be preferred to plenty, though perhaps the power was sought with a view to plenty. The mercantilists saw little chance of mutual gain; the plenty of one nation must be gained at the expense of others.

[6] V. I. Lenin, *Imperialism: The Highest Stage of Capitalism* (Petrograd, 1917; English edition, Martin-Lawrence, London, 1933).

[7] J. A. Hobson, *Imperialism, a Study* (London, 1905).

There followed the "liberal" era with emphasis on plenty and on the mutual benefit of trade. Plenty required peace, and mutually profitable trade was expected to promote international peace. Adam Smith had said:

Commerce, which ought naturally to be, among nations, as among individuals, a bond of union and friendship, has become the most fertile source of discord and animosity. The capricious ambition of kings and ministers has not, during the present and preceding century, been more fatal to the repose of Europe than the impertinent jealousy of merchants and manufacturers.[8]

Cobden and Gladstone, a century later, still hoped that free trade (which requires peace as a condition) would contribute to peace. Their error, as Lionel Robbins says in *The Economic Causes of War*,[9] was in their failure to notice the "absence of the rule of law" in the international sphere.

The Cobdenite liberals would have never dreamt of urging that, within national areas, the long-run interests of the majority in peaceful co-operation could be regarded as secured without a framework of law and coercion. Such a view would have been the view, not of liberals, but of philosophical anarchists. What justification had they, therefore, for assuming that, in the relations between the inhabitants of different national areas, a superior harmony might be expected?[10]

Free trade did not spread as Cobden had hoped; restrictionism and exclusion from colonial markets by some forced those who did not practice restrictionism into further territorial acquisition. The resultant bickering gives some basis for the Marxist-Leninist explanation of World Wars I and II; but it is not convincing. It is particularly unconvincing in putting capitalism rather than nationalism as the cause of war. If it was unconvincing in 1939, it is much more so now. We have seen socialist nations exploiting colonial territories (or satellites) on a scale unprecedented in the history of modern capitalism; we have seen the cost of armaments rise to a point where no conceivable economic gain from the exercise of power could be considered worth the financial cost, still less the "human" cost; we have developed confidence that we can enjoy under capitalism an extraordinarily high standard of living in spite of the restrictions and

---

[8] Adam Smith, *Wealth of Nations* (New York, 1937), p. 460.
[9] Lionel Robbins, *The Economic Causes of War* (London, 1939).
[10] *Ibid.*, pp. 99-100.

exclusions to which we may be exposed, and without the exploitation of others of which we are suspect; we have shown our willingness to aid in the development of the "colonial" peoples by gift and loan and technical aid; we have entered an era when limited war for minor objectives carries such a threat of global, nuclear war that no economic advantage could justify the risk. Yet we are still pictured as "imperialist" and our "capitalism" is seen by the other half of the world as something not just distasteful, but as warlike in its essence. If the mercantilists sought power for plenty, and the liberals sought plenty independently of power, we now need plenty for power to prevent the submergence of our civilization; plenty for power for defense, power to dam the rising tide which would overwhelm us; not power for expansion and for the overwhelming of others. We need plenty to demonstrate that our freer way of life can provide it (and we must make clear that leisure is one of the goods we have in plenty). We need plenty to enable us to contribute to the development of others. The affluent society cannot relax; but the affluent society should take seriously to heart Galbraith's warning that plenty for defense can only be made available by a highly productive society that can quickly turn from the habits of affluence to the habits of austerity.[11] A "high" standard of living requires the productivity that gives plenty, but also the judgment that assures that plenty of the right things; our survival depends on the quality of this judgment and on our adaptability in emergency as much as on the excellence of our technology, the quantity of our capital and the skill of our labor.

So far as the United States and the Commonwealth are concerned there is little of imperialism left; our consciences can be relatively clear and we may hope that the Communist caricature will come to be recognized as such. But if we do not plot consciously the exploitation of our neighbors, we do unconscious injury by domestic policies the external effect of which we ignore. Here a Canadian, a citizen of a country heavily dependent economically on the United States yet big enough for its own actions to have important repercussions on other countries, is particularly sensitive. It is a commonplace that economic stability, or stable high level employment, is essential for the stability, and determination, of the Western Alliance. It is a commonplace that responsibility for stability in this trading world

[11] John Kenneth Galbraith, The Affluent Society (Boston, 1958). See especially chap. xii, "The Illusion of National Security," pp. 161-180.

lies very heavily on the United States. By independent action Canada can do something to insulate itself against fluctuations in the economy of the United States. However, by and large the fortunes of Canada are determined by the behavior of the American economy. We, a nearly affluent society, can afford the loss of income of a recession more easily than the poorer countries; but the politically tolerable level of unemployment in Canada, as in most countries, is becoming very small. We cannot convert, or keep converted, to a free system nations who see their progress to plenty stopped by a United States recession, and who face the discontents of an army of unemployed. The Marxists' story of the contradictions of capitalism becomes impressive; the continuing affluence of the United States in recession cannot offset this impression.

It is not enough to emphasize the responsibility for maintaining high level employment; it is necessary also to remember that we must not promote our own stability by exporting our unemployment. Nor is this just a matter of general policies in the face of general recession; it is also a matter of particular adjustments in particular industries and regions. The protection of one vested interest after another in our countries means the infliction of one injury after another on a weaker group in a country on whose loyalty to the common cause we count. We in Canada have felt the effects of such policies practised by you; we can take it though we will protest and with some justification. But I speak here, out of our experience, to remind you of what you do to others, more vulnerable than we. I urge you to remember that the distinction between domestic and international affairs is largely unreal. And I must add that our own skirts are not clean.

Now this leads to another observation. We, the affluent and not-so-affluent nations, can make considerable sacrifices for the common cause, for defense and for aid, as long as the burden is evenly distributed. What we cannot accept is unemployment. From Mr. Gaddis Smith's paper on Canadian experience in World War I you will remember the discussion of Sir Robert Borden's difficulties; the problem was not the over-all financial burden of the war but the number unemployed. I remind you of Borden's cable: "A very painful and even bitter feeling is being aroused throughout the Dominion. Men are going without bread in Canada while those across the line are receiving wages for work that could be done as efficiently and as cheaply in this country."[12] Unemployment reduces the plenty out of which any contribution must be made; but more seriously, it concentrates the burden of sacrifice on the unemployed whose real distress is aggravated by the frustration of individual idleness when national effort is so clearly needed. We must learn much more about the treatment of unemployment; surely we must provide more adequate unemployment pay (have we really caught up with the postwar inflation in this regard?); we must do more in retraining and relocation of displaced workers; we must be readier to compensate those injured in the process by which plenty increases for the society as a whole. Only if we learn these things can we adjust our domestic economies to changes in the pattern of world trade as the new countries develop. Only if we learn these things can we abolish that most unreasonable fear of "gifts," or that fear of cheap goods which makes a "trade offensive" by the U.S.S.R. a threat! Must we always look on cheap goods as a danger rather than a boon? Is it not cheapness and plenty that we seek? And only if we learn these things can we laugh at the "threat" of disarmament. That disarmament could spell distress rather than almost unimaginable plenty; that a clever U.S.S.R. could by a disarmament agreement win a bloodless victory; these are propositions with just enough truth to be worrying. But the worry is largely that the United States would resolve its own problem by domestic policies which would intensify the difficulty of adjustment for the rest of the world. Surely we could adjust to the change so as to increase the plenty and leisure of the Western World and to contribute on a vast scale to the increase of the wealth of the have-not nations.

In the nineteenth century the industrial countries of Western Europe contributed on a vast scale to the development of our two countries, first by providing a market for our product, second by lending capital. Did this constitute "exploitation"? If so, one can only say that the exploited flourished remarkably! What then of this last half of the twentieth century? There is no doubt in my mind that we must give aid on a much greater scale than we at present contemplate. (Our Canadian contribution is currently of the order of $60,000,000 a year. We cannot be very proud of this.) But concentration on "aid" is dangerous if it means obsession with the division of the pie while inadequate attention is paid to the problems

[12] See above p. 39.

of increasing its size. And one must remember that "transfers" have not been politically easy between groups within one nation between which strong sympathy exists based on contiguity, common culture, and shared history. We cannot in inflationary days pretend that our gifts to foreign countries are costless; we must give, and accept the cost. But because this will not be politically easy, we must be particularly concerned to develop the conditions under which the least aid is needed. This was the wise message of Sir Dennis Robertson when he addressed the Bicentennial Conference at Columbia University on *National Policy for Economic Welfare at Home and Abroad.*

Neither we nor anybody else seems to be at all ready to practise on an international scale such a degree of emotional solidarity as prevails, in spite of differences of interest, between, say, London and Yorkshire, or between the Atlantic Coast and the Middle West. This being so, it is of high importance that the economic arrangements of nations and between nations should be so designed as to minimize the making of chronic and possibly unmeetable calls on the limited stocks of international altruism. That, of course, is the idea behind the slogan, "Trade, not aid" in which the demands now being made upon the United States by other Western Nations have been epitomized. . . . What we ask, if fully accorded, would result in shifts of activity which, we believe, would be to the advantage of the United States as a whole, but which would undoubtedly impair the earning power and dislocate the lives of an appreciable number of blameless American citizens.[18]

Sir Dennis would rely on "unexhausted reserves of generosity and willingness to share" as an "iron ration in times of emergency or unforeseen setback." I would hope that we would extend our aid beyond our present level; but with Sir Dennis, I have more confidence in the good effect on the "developing" countries of a strong market for their products in affluent societies than in unlimited international altruism.

2.

In conclusion I want to say a few words about two peripheral problems. First, I want to express my concern as an economist at our ineffectiveness in the war of ideas. It is not enough to be against communism; we must be for something and it is not enough to say

[18] R. Lekachman, ed., *National Policy for Economic Welfare at Home and Abroad* (New York, 1955). Chap. i, "What Does the Economist Economize?" is by Sir Dennis Robertson. See p. 4.

that we are for "our way of life" if we cannot explain to ourselves, to our young people, and to our allies what this involves. Now, I realize that no mere economist can be expected to provide an adequate statement; but this economist feels that the economic elements in that statement are often inadequately expressed. "Free enterprise" may appeal to the few who have become, or see a chance of becoming, entrepreneurs; to them, too, "laissez faire" may be attractive. But have these slogans much appeal compared with the apparent reasonableness of "planning"? Must we not explain the liberal economics? In particular, three points must be made. First, we must make it clear that the ends of the socialist and of the liberal are, in large part, the same; both seek economic welfare. They differ as to means and as to the relative weight to be attached to the economic and noneconomic elements in welfare, on the value, for instance, of freedom. Neither has a monopoly of the sense of justice or concern for the welfare of the people. There is a wide gulf between this economic liberalism and what I would call "economic royalism" which would insist on the right of the entrepreneur to exploit as he wished. Second, we must discuss frankly the role of self-interest, making clear the effectiveness of the individual pursuit of wealth in promoting the increase of social wealth. Alfred Marshall, who preached on other occasions the virtues of economic chivalry, noted "that progress chiefly depends on the extent to which the *strongest* and not merely the *highest* forces of human nature can be utilised for the increase of the social good." For a long time to come, I believe, self-interest, the profit motive widely interpreted, will provide the "steam" in the economy. We forget this at our peril. The Soviet Union has not forgotten it. But too many of us are in danger of becoming ashamed of self-seeking long before we become so capable of unselfish public service that economic chivalry will guarantee the drive for increasing productivity that the profit motive has achieved and is continuing to achieve. To go back to the quotation from Marshall, let us not ignore the phrase "utilised for the increase of the social good" as we worry about our inability to achieve the heights of pure unselfishness. Third, we must make explicit the importance of the social, cultural, ethical, and legal framework as conditions for the effectiveness of economic freedom in achieving economic welfare. The emphasis on self-interest does not mean a belief in unregulated free enterprise, but it means a belief in harnessing self-interest by appropriate regulation to the public good rather than dispensing with this motive power and seeking an alternative source of power.[14]   There is, as the late Henry Simons said, a "positive program of laissez faire."[15]   Even more neglected than the framework of law and government regulation has been the ethical framework.   O. H. Taylor, in several essays in his *Economics and Liberalism*,[16] has demonstrated that the great founders of the liberal tradition recognized these "conditions."   We need to rediscover them.   Let me quote two sentences from Taylor's essays:

. . . Smith agreed with Shaftesbury that self-centred economic ambition is socially beneficent, *so long as* it is limited, as it normally is, by the beneficent dictates of our moral faculties.[17]

Competition could work as Adam Smith thought it should work only in a society whose legal system, and whose current and effective standards of business morality, were products of the effective working of the force of sympathy.[18]

Finally, we should remember that perfection is unattainable, and that we are seeking the better of alternative imperfect systems.   It is perhaps not quite unreasonable to add a warning against comparing communism as it might be at its ideal best with capitalism at its worst, or *vice versa*.   We must try to look at each as it is and as it seems to be becoming.

The second of my peripheral problems is related to my experience as a "professor" rather than as an economist.   I can do no more than raise it for discussion for I do not know how real a problem it is, how general a problem, how serious a problem.   And in the limited area in which I have encountered it I do not know what to do about it.   The problem is this: Do we by our treatment of the students who come to our universities from other countries strengthen, or weaken, the ties which bind our alliance?   We provide much useful training, know-how which must increase the potentiality for plenty in many lands.   But do they go back with added respect for our "way of life"?   Are we exposing them to unnecessary frustration by putting them into

[14] See my paper, "Some Reflections on the Classical Literature of Political Economy" in *Studia Varia*, ed. E. G. D. Murray, published for the Royal Society of Canada (Toronto, 1957) pp. 71-85.

[15] Henry Simons, *Economic Policy for a Free Society* (Chicago, 1948), chap. ii.

[16] O. H. Taylor, *Economics and Liberalism: Collected Papers* (Cambridge, Massachusetts, 1955).

[17] *Ibid.*, p. 30.   [18] *Ibid.*, p. 97.

an educational mill devised for our own people? Are we ready enough to adapt our requirements and our curricula to the special needs of these visitors? Perhaps this is a special problem for the social sciences, for these "sciences" in any of our countries are to a high degree culture bound. Perhaps it is a problem for the community in which our university exists, for along with the liberal acceptance of the foreigner on the campus may go unhappy experiences of exclusion and discrimination in the community. Perhaps the trouble is that the traffic is too nearly one way; more of us should go, not as tourists, but as students and teachers to live in the universities of our allies. Nor is this a matter of interchange between countries of widely differing culture. A recent visit to Toronto by Professor Perroux of the Collège de France emphasized, while it helped to break down, the barriers which cut us off from the culture of France; we hope that two-way traffic in economics will develop between Paris and Toronto. As we add to the staff of the Department of Political Economy students of Asian and African affairs we may make progress not only in the understanding of the problems of those parts of the world, but we may also be making some contribution to the solution of the problem I have raised. Meanwhile, in Toronto a voluntary organization, Friendly Relations with Overseas Students (F.R.O.S.), does valiant work for individual students, and develops some of the "warmth" which is sadly missing in our alliance for "cold war."

8

A Middle Power in the Cold War

Edgar McInnis

Like most other lands, Canada finds her policies conditioned by her structure and her history. Her national interests grow out of her economic framework and her internal social and political balance; their expression is affected by sentiments and traditions whose roots reach back into earlier centuries. The structure may change as the nation develops. The traditions may be modified as new conditions call for new responses. But, short of total catastrophe, the social and economic bases of a nation are never completely wiped out by technological changes or even by political revolutions, and the past imposes its continuity on the successive adaptations that are expressed in changing policies.

A nation's policies are also conditioned by environment. No country is so completely self-contained that it can avoid the need to project its national interests beyond its own borders in the effort to realize its national purposes. Yet there are limits to its ability to impose its own aspirations on the rest of the world. Other nations have different sets of interests that they are not ready to abandon, and one of the tasks of foreign policy is to take the maximum advantage of favorable opportunities in the world situation, and to reduce to the minimum the effects of adverse factors on the country's own national development. In this field, too, there is the constant need to adapt to changing conditions. The economic situation of a particular country may be drastically altered by the development of new trade routes that bypass old entrepôts or the appearance of new products that tend to supersede old staples. Its political and strategic position can be changed by the decline of old empires and the rise of new super-states, or the development of new weapons that pose new security problems. Yet here also there is seldom a complete ex-

punging of the old lines of external policy or a comprehensive sever-
ance of traditional friendships and connections.

The story of Canada's postwar foreign policy is one of adaptation
to these two sets of factors, domestic and external. It is possibly the
latter that has called for the more drastic adjustments. Domestic
evolution has been striking in many ways, but changes in the fundamental pattern have perhaps been less revolutionary than the up-
heavals in the general world balance. Yet the repercussions of world
events have had their effects on Canada's internal conditions and outlook, adding their weight to the effect of changes in the domestic
sphere; and these in their turn have reacted on the conduct of foreign
policy and the attitude toward world issues.

There are two essential facts about Canada's structure that retain
their historic validity even in the present day. Socially and politically,
she is conditioned by the continued existence of a dual culture and a
dual language. Economically, she still relies to a very large extent
on the production of natural staples for sale in the world markets.
In both respects there have, of course, been very real changes from
even a generation ago. The significance of cultural divisions has
altered and in some respects undoubtedly diminished. The range of
natural products has broadened; some have risen in importance while
others have declined; new elements of maturity have been added to
the economy in such sectors as processing and transportation. These
are factors that modify the form in which Canada's national interests
can best be expressed or implemented; they do not essentially alter
the ultimate roots from which those interests spring.

In this area the most pertinent change of all arose from the change
of status that had been achieved during the interwar years. Emergence into nationhood had been a gradual process, and even after the
formal barriers to independent action had been removed, the habits
and attitudes of the colonial era were slow to disappear. These in-
hibiting influences were largely swept away by World War II.
Canada emerged as a nation in her own right, with a sense of her
separate identity and her equal place in the ranks of the other sovereign members of the world community. She had become aware of
the privileges and opportunities of nationhood; she had come by
experience to realize also its responsibilities. If there were restraining considerations, they no longer arose from legal limitations as
such (even though these may have had their lingering psychological

legacies) but from a sense of the limited influence that a nation of Canada's capacities could exert on world politics. Within that framework there was a new sense of national self-confidence that found expression in active and constructive efforts in the field of foreign policy.

Along with this, and expressing the new attitudes that developed with a growing sense of national identity, there emerged new figures to shape the form and substance of Canadian external policy. Mackenzie King had been concerned with the protracted struggle to free Canada from external controls. For a quarter of a century he had fought the battle for full independence in the sphere of external relations. He had become habituated to look with distaste on the restraining effects of any outside commitments, not merely toward the empire which orbited around Westminster, but almost equally toward the world collective system with its center in Geneva. Freedom of national decision was his cardinal objective in external affairs, and having gained this from London, he had no inclination to accept any diminution of such freedom in the name of collective action.

His successors typified the evolution of the Canadian outlook as it adapted itself to changing world conditions. Louis St. Laurent became the first man to hold as a separate office the Secretaryship of State for External Affairs. An internationalist in the classic liberal tradition, he entered upon his ministry at a time when the aggressive policy of the Soviet Union revealed unmistakably the rising totalitarian threat to democratic freedoms throughout the world. His response was based on a conviction that free nations must stand together to preserve their liberties, and that Canada, whose national security was bound up with that of the other Western democracies, must make her contribution and subordinate her right of unhampered decision to the needs of the common cause.

This was the approach that was developed to fruition by Lester Pearson. He was by no means the sole contributor to the evolution of Canada's postwar policy. Political decisions were intimately bound up with other vital aspects such as finance and trade, production and defense. The ministers in charge of these departments under St. Laurent as Prime Minister were vigorous personalities who were usually ready to fight for their own views in opposition to their colleagues when occasion arose. Yet, while there might be sharp differences on specific questions, there was a broad consensus on over-all objectives, and this was embodied and implemented through the policies of Lester Pearson as the architect of Canada's postwar external relations, which reached their mature form under his direction.

For Canada, as for the other Western democracies, the dominating fact was the cold war with its inherent threat to world peace and stability. The territorial conquests of communism, backed as they were by the massive military strength of the Soviet Union, would if unchecked bring the destruction of the kind of world in which Canada as a free democracy could hope to survive and prosper. Physical force was needed to contain Soviet aggression, and this meant the creation of a military balance of power with the attendant risk of armed conflict resulting in a third world war. Canada's position, if she were involved in such a war, would be much more vulnerable than in previous conflicts. Her virtual immunity from direct attack had been wiped out by the advent of the nuclear-rocket age. Her ultimate security was bound up with that of the Free World, yet participation in the defense of strategic areas beyond her own borders would expose her to new hazards and exact a new and formidable price.

In the interwar years there had developed a certain current of neutralist opinion in Canada though it never rose to major significance. In the postwar period only a shadowy remnant survived. Even the divergence between the two main racial groups, previously so acute in the field of external affairs, virtually disappeared. There was no longer ground for the suspicion that Canada was being dragged into a conflict on behalf of British imperial ambitions, or for the illusion, which in the thirties had induced a wilful blindness toward the brutal menace of Nazism, that militarism could be induced to yield to reason and totalitarianism enlisted in the defense of Christian civilization. The enemy was clearly identified and clearly recognized as an enemy, and French-speaking Catholic Canadians were certainly not behind their English-speaking Protestant compatriots in their resolve to resist the threat to the foundations of the society to which they were so deeply attached.

The result was a national consensus on basic objectives that gave concrete substance to Canada's new sense of national self-confidence as Canadians became habituated to the realities of national independence. Internally, the foundations were laid for the development of a positive foreign policy; external conditions called for positive decisions in a way that was almost inescapable. Canada found herself impelled by the demands of the postwar situation into an active and sustained role in world affairs. The nature of the existing balance was clear. The need to maintain it on a favorable level was urgent. The obligation to make a contribution to this end commensurate with the national resources was one which practically all Canadians accepted as necessary and inevitable.

Given this agreement as to ends, the means of attaining them became consequently restricted to a relatively narrow range of choice. Canada could hardly hope by her own unaided efforts to mould the scheme of things to her heart's desire. In her direct contacts with other countries she could press her own interests on her own initiative; in the wider sphere of world politics, she could make little impression by trying to go it alone. To attain her objectives, she must be ready to act with other like-minded states who shared her basic aims. Foremost among such states were her traditional associates, Britain and the United States. In that respect the historical continuity of her external policies was carried on unbroken into the postwar era. At the same time, the new conditions called for new adaptations. The relative weight given to these two major partners tended to change; the wider scope of the new problems called for wider associations; and the consequences of Canada's maturing independence were reflected in modifications of her attitude toward the leadership that she had earlier looked for from the United Kingdom and the ascendancy in world affairs more recently acquired by the United States.

This last element in particular was illustrated by the emergent concept of Canada as a Middle Power. She was no longer content to act simply as an auxiliary to one or other of the larger nations in the realm of external affairs. Her policies were her own, based on a reasoned concept of her own national interest; and while they coincided in the main with those of the other democracies, especially the English-speaking ones, she held herself free to assert her own point of view when policies diverged. Yet dissent was bound to be limited by practical considerations, and not least by the realization that a refusal to act with others might leave her impotent to take any effective action at all.

As between impotence and acquiescence, the desirable thing seemed to be the attainment of a recognized right of influence over decisions affecting Canada's interests and obligations. While she could not pretend to the stature of a Great Power, she was reluctant to be lumped together with all the smaller ones. She had greater resources than most of them; she was expected in a crisis to make a much greater contribution to the common cause. The war had called forth an effort second only to those of the Great Powers, and the demands of peace might be equally exacting. What she aspired to was a degree of influence comparable to the scale of her participation. It looked for a time as though the battle for status that Canada had successfully waged within the Commonwealth would be carried into the wider sphere of the community of nations.

In actual fact, of course, this aim was never pressed to a formal issue. The tentative effort to get the Middle Powers recognized as a special category within the United Nations failed at San Francisco, and any hope of attaining it as a general feature of the international structure was soon tacitly abandoned. Not only was there certain to be controversy over what states should be admitted to the ranks. There was the more operative consideration that the line was almost impossible to draw on a basis of either distinct interests or separate functions. There were relatively few cases in which the interests that were pursued by the middle-sized nations were distinct in character from those of their associates, small as well as great. There were a few cases—for example, the commissions that supervised the settlement in Indo-China, or the agreements on the composition of the United Nations Emergency Force—where distrust of the larger states and lack of resources on the part of the smaller ones imposed a special role on the Middle Powers; but such instances were relatively few and did not lead to any clear-cut division that would give the middle states a separate and clearly recognized position.

Yet the fact remained that Canada faced a real dilemma when it came to reconciling the range of her external involvements with her available means for implementing them. Isolated voices have occasionally been raised to urge that Canada should stand aloof from specific commitments in favor of a policy of non-alignment. In theory at least this would leave her free to formulate her own independent policies on particular issues as they arose, to decide the type of action that she could most effectively take in any given situation, and to use her potential weight in the power balance as a leverage on the side of moderation and compromise. This tends to ignore the extent to which Canada is in practice committed by the very nature of her interests to the common cause of the Free World as a whole, and to overrate her ability to exercise pressure based on an assumed freedom of choice that does not in fact exist, at least so far as fundamental issues are concerned. The alternative is to accept the facts of life, to recognize that Canada must join in a common effort on behalf of common aims, and to be reconciled to the secondary position that she will in consequence find allocated to her in the councils of the world community.

If the choice of the second of these alternatives has been almost instinctive on the part of the Canadian people as a whole, it also finds solid support from sound practical considerations. Soviet communism is a threat to the existence of the democratic society with which Canada's own vital interests are inescapably bound up. The threat cannot be met by individual nations acting independently, or even by the Great Powers among the democracies acting in concert. The full collaboration of all interested nations is needed if an effective balance is to be created and maintained; and Canada, unable in this situation to assure her national interests by her own unaided resources, has inevitably been impelled to look to a collective system within which those resources can be utilized with cumulative effect.

One result is that the United Nations bulks larger as an operative factor in Canadian foreign policy than did the League of Nations in the years between the wars. There was a genuine attraction to the principles behind the League, to the concept of a world organization as a remedy for international anarchy, but this was accompanied by a reluctance to entrust to a collection of foreigners the right to exercise any portion of Canada's newly won sovereignty. In the end there was an equal reluctance on the part of the Canadian government itself to take action in the name of international law and order that might embroil it with other states, however deplorable their conduct might be in defiance of the letter and spirit of the covenant. Aversion to the use of sanctions, pious reliance on moral force, and an increasingly stubborn clinging to the policy of non-commitment were the main features of Canada's attitude toward the collective system on the eve of World War II.

The inadequacy of such an approach was made all too plain by the outcome. If peace was to be sought through a world organization—and this was an aspiration to which the appalling experience of the war gave fresh urgency—a necessary minimum of power must be devolved on such organization by the member states. It was evident that the main strength must come in the first instance from the Great Powers. This was recognized by Canadian political leaders, but they were not satisfied with the prospect of a system that would leave the right of decision as well as the obligation of action solely in the hands of the larger states. If power and responsibility were to go together, as Mackenzie King asserted, then a secondary state such as Canada was entitled to a voice in decisions commensurate with the demands that she would be expected to meet. The converse of this was the recognition that Canada must be ready to make a contribution commensurate with her resources if her claim to an adequate voice in decisions was to be justified. There was little dissent from the logic of this proposition. "The Canadian people," said Mr. St. Laurent, "wish Canada to be a part of the international organization and to do whatever may be required in order to be a full partner in it. I believe that whatever may be required is a price that Canada is prepared to pay to make the organization effective, if it can be made effective."

This is not to say that Canada was yet prepared to subordinate her right of independent decision wholly to the authority of an international body. Indeed, it would be hard to find any sovereign nation that was willing to submit its destinies to the dictates of a world superstate. What can fairly be claimed is that Canada does not lag behind other member states in her readiness to strengthen the direct authority of the United Nations in matters concerned with the prevention of aggression and the peaceful settlement of disputes, and that she has repeatedly shown her willingness to join in co-operating with the organization and with her fellow-members in actions that are calculated to contribute to world peace and stability.

This attitude has been consistently maintained through all the vicissitudes that have beset the United Nations since its foundation. There has been a measure of disappointment over the failure of the organization to fulfil all the hopes that were initially placed in it, a certain disillusionment about its capacity to achieve the aims for which it was designed; there has been little tendency to abandon it as wholly ineffective or to discard it as an instrument for the advancement of world order. On the contrary, there has been a continued emphasis on the United Nations as a major area of Canada's interests and activity. If its limitations have been made evident by experience, they have been accepted realistically; and far from leading to luke-warmness or indifference, they have if anything increased Canada's concern to strengthen the positive and constructive elements that the United Nations organization still contains. The weakness of the League was made an excuse for a policy of wary aloofness and the avoidance of commitments. It is symptomatic of Canada's advance in national maturity and self-confidence that the deficiencies of the United Nations have had almost the opposite effect, and that Canada, instead of trying to evade her responsibilities under the Charter, has been prepared to fulfil and even to extend them in a number of significant respects.

To no small degree, indeed, it is participation in the work of the United Nations that on the one hand enables Canada to develop the advantages that attach to her position as a Middle Power and, on the other hand, illustrates the limitations inherent in such a position. The United Nations, and particularly the Assembly, represents diplomacy by conference organized on a continuing basis. Up to a point this gives an opportunity to a secondary power to make a larger impact than is usual through the kind of bilateral contacts that are customary in conventional diplomacy, to win the trust and respect of other states, and thus to increase its influence over major decisions in which it is concerned. This is particularly evident in cases where neither the Great Powers nor the smaller states are appropriate instruments for dealing with some important international issue. In such cases, and especially where the issue is vested with a colonial aspect, Canada ranks with India and the Scandinavian countries as the states that are normally called on to make a leading and a constructive contribution. When economic matters are in question, the combination of states is somewhat different, but here too Canada is in the forefront because of her advanced technology and standard of living and her ability to provide capital assistance on a scale second only to that of the larger Powers. Yet the need to accept these obligations is accompanied by only a limited capacity to lay down the conditions under which they shall be implemented. Canada's aid may be important and desirable in a given situation; it is rarely so indispensable that other states can be pressured into following Canada's lead against their better judgment or to their apparent individual disadvantage. In the Suez crisis, for example, Canada was able to play a leading part in the establishment of UNEF. Her best efforts were not enough to secure the creation of a permanent stand-by force as a regular instrument for dealing with future crises, or even to get a determined and concerted attempt at a final settlement of the Middle East problem that had bedeviled world politics for the past decade.

The positive side of Canadian foreign policy, and the accompanying willingness to accept increased external obligations, are even more strikingly apparent when we turn to the North Atlantic Treaty Organization. Here is a concrete illustration of the contrast between Canada's prewar and postwar attitudes toward external commitments. The decline of the League resulted in an apprehensive aloofness from all such engagements, whether under the Covenant or through promises of support to other Powers, including the United Kingdom. The frustrations of the United Nations in the sphere of security led, not to a discouraged resignation, but to a determined search for an effective alternative that would fill the resulting gap, and to an equally resolute acceptance of the burdens that must be borne as a consequence of Canada's participation as a full member of NATO.

In a sense, NATO was an extension of Canada's traditional connections and her long-standing interest in a favorable world balance. Twice within a generation Canada had been drawn into major conflicts born of authoritarian and militaristic threats to the democratic way of life. The security of Western Europe was clearly essential as a bulwark for the kind of world in which Canada could hope to survive and prosper. The United Kingdom was a bastion that must be maintained if Western Europe was to be preserved. The strength and resources of the United States must be enlisted if democratic resistance was to command the necessary power, as well as the confidence and resolution without which the will to resist might all too readily be dissipated. When Mr. St. Laurent, in 1948, called for the creation by the nations of the Free World of "an overwhelming preponderance of force over any adversary or combination of adversaries," he made it clear that this was to be "under the leadership of Great Britain, the United States and France," and in fact the support of at least the first two of these Powers was essential in Canadian eyes for any effective system of collective security.

At the same time, Canada's participation in NATO was something more than simply a new expression of an old-standing orientation. Right up to 1939, Britain was the touchstone for Canada's attitude toward the European balance. If Britain stayed aloof from a European conflict, it was quite inconceivable that Canada should plunge into the hostilities. If Britain were drawn into a major war, it was virtually impossible for Canada to stay out. The latter situation still obtained, for the survival of the United Kingdom remained vital to Canada's national interests. But Western Europe was also vital, and Canada's entry into NATO was an explicit recognition of this salient fact. Her participation in European affairs was no longer remote and indirect, dependent on her connection with Britain; it was direct and immediate as a full partner in a common enterprise on behalf of Western security.

Two factors of special significance were inherent in this development. The first was the emergence of the United States from a long-standing tradition of isolation to the assumption of an active world leadership. Quite apart from the fact that this provided the Atlantic alliance with the solid core around which the other members could rally, it also released Canada from her prewar dilemma of reconciling her policy with divergent attitudes on the part of the United Kingdom and the United States. The two countries were now close partners in world politics, and with this fact as an established base, Canada was enabled to look beyond her most immediate connections and to frame her policies with broader considerations in view.

The second aspect was the change that has already been mentioned in the area of domestic opinion, particularly in French Canada. If on the one hand the continuance of co-operation with Britain through NATO gratified those groups in English-speaking Canada who still cherished the idea of the imperial connection, on the other hand Canada's independent membership in a wider grouping removed the stigma of subservience to Westminster that had previously been a chief ground for French-Canadian opposition to external commitments. Canada's entry into NATO was clearly and unquestionably a strictly Canadian decision based on a conception of Canada's own national interests to which all major groups within the country subscribed.

In effect, what resulted was a new departure, of major significance as a stage in the evolution of Canadian foreign policy, yet growing out of considerations that were traditional as well as basic. The North Atlantic region had always been for Canada an area of primary concern. This was implicit in her constant efforts to harmonize her policies with those of both Britain and the United States. Now that a solid basis for harmony had been achieved, the wider interest could become explicit in its expression. It was an adaptation of historic factors to the demands of a new situation; and with the establishment of NATO, Canada's longest-standing external connections were supplemented and rounded out in the regional grouping that was henceforth a major pivot of Canada's approach to world affairs.

The postwar years saw a comparable adjustment in Canada's attitude toward another grouping that also represented a major and traditional interest. The Commonwealth of Nations was now undergoing a striking transformation. The emergence of the old Commonwealth during the interwar period—a development to which Canada had made a leading contribution—had set in motion forces that were having ever-broadening effects. The new Commonwealth that evolved after the war was different in composition, different in outlook, and involved considerable adjustments in the attitude toward the structure of the Commonwealth as an institution.

The relationship that was established by the Balfour Report and the Statute of Westminster left Canada's aspirations very largely satisfied. Her persistent aim had been to achieve for Canada the unqualified right to manage her own affairs, external as well as internal. This involved a rejection of any centralized machinery that might conceivably result in the subordination of separate and independent decisions to the concensus of other Commonwealth members, or even more distasteful, to the overriding weight of the Mother Country. It was a struggle for sovereign status as the basis for a continuing connection, and this absorbed Canada's efforts to the virtual exclusion of other aspects. There was relatively little attention devoted to the question of the composition of the Commonwealth. There was, of course, the anticipation that India would in due course take her place on an equal footing with other members. There was also a tendency to assume that the existing members would continue to stick together, and a genuine regret when Ireland decided to sever her Commonwealth connection. In addition, there was an almost automatic tendency to look at the Commonwealth through the perspective of Britain as the center and the motive force. There was a sentiment of fraternity with the other fellow-Dominions, a desire to retain the sense of united purpose and outlook that the Commonwealth seemed to provide; there was relatively little direct contact for specific common purposes with Australia or New Zealand or South

Africa, and relatively little feeling of close and continuous co-operation except in matters in which co-operation with Britain on the part of each individual Dominion was the central motivating factor.

There is reason to believe that Canada would have been prepared to see this situation continue indefinitely. It was a pattern that met her concept of a settled and satisfactory relationship, and she had little or no incentive to press for further changes. The changes that came about in the postwar period were the result of pressures from other quarters, from newer or even from still aspiring members as they emerged from colonial status. But if Canada played no part in initiating the new advance, she did nothing to hamper it. Her attitude was one of benevolence toward other embryo nations who were moving along the path that Canada had pioneered, of approval for Britain's far-sighted policy in conceding a broadening measure of freedom to her former dependencies in response to the rising demands of nationalism, and even of complacence toward the formal changes in the structural and symbolic aspects of the Commonwealth that accompanied the new advance.

There can be little doubt that the dynamic and dramatic new phase that began with the admission of the new Asian states to full membership resulted in a fresh upsurge of interest in the Commonwealth on the part of a considerable section of the Canadian public. There remained, of course, an underlying attachment to the British connection, and to the Commonwealth as an emanation of Britain's imperial greatness. At this level, however, there was a tendency to take the existing relationship for granted and to bring it under discussion chiefly when it looked as though events were threatening to weaken that connection in its economic or political aspects. But there was a second and newer level from which the extension of the principle of free association to the countries of Asia and Africa was viewed much more in the light of its bearing on the world struggle to uphold the ideals of freedom and democracy than from the narrower point of view of its significance for Britain's power position. From this aspect, the Commonwealth appeared as a unique instrument for maintaining the links between Asia and the West, a bridge between the Western democracies and the uncommitted nations that were of such potential importance for the world balance, a means for creating a sense of common interest and establishing an awareness of common ideals. Canadians who were hardly concerned over whether Canada had any influence in Australia and who had long ago given up any idea that Canada could exert any influence over the Nationalist government in South Africa were urgently desirous that every effort be made to establish close and friendly contacts with India and to show generosity and helpfulness toward the newer Commonwealth members. In these cases, Britain was no longer looked on as the normal intermediary. There were positive attempts to form direct links that would establish Canada as a friend in her own right and as a Western nation to whom the newer states could freely extend their trust and friendship in return. And if these objectives were incompatible with the concept of unity based on common allegiance, as laid down in the Balfour Report, then Canada was prepared to see the older conventions adapted to the new conditions, to accept the disappearance of the Common Crown as the necessary price for holding the newer members in continued association, and to help in working out the formula that enabled those members to replace the monarchy by a republican regime and still remain within the Commonwealth.

Thus, while the North Atlantic stood out as the prime area of Canada's interests and activities, her Commonwealth connection resulted in a wider geographical involvement and a selective extension of her external associations. Even further, her membership in the United Nations opened world-wide horizons and symbolized her inescapable concern with world affairs in their broadest sense. Her national interests were bound up with world peace and stability. She might have no direct stake in internal developments in Egypt or Indonesia, but when repercussions from those developments threatened to disturb the international economy or the existing political balance, Canada could hardly remain indifferent.

At the same time, there was a natural desire to refrain from getting involved in areas of purely general and indirect concern. There were limits to Canada's material resources, and perhaps even more, as a middle-sized state, to her resources in personnel. The burden of her existing commitments was far from negligible in relation to her size and capacities. It seemed in principle desirable to concentrate her efforts on those areas where her interests were most immediate and where her contribution would be most effective. It was with reluctance and at times with considerable perturbation that Canada found herself compelled by circumstances to extend her direct activities to spheres with which she was unfamiliar and from which she had previously been able to stand aloof.

Here was an illustration of the obligations consequent on participation in collective activities under the conditions created by the post-war balance of power. Great Powers as well as smaller ones found their main strength pinned down at the points of maximum danger and had limited resources to spare for secondary areas. It could no longer be taken for granted that they would in all circumstances assume a unilateral obligation to maintain stability in specific regions, even in ones in which they had special interests. This was accentuated when situations arose in which, for political reasons, it was desirable to exclude the Great Powers from participation in special arrangements. Taken together, these factors meant that other nations must be prepared to assume obligations in cases that the larger states would previously have dealt with on their own initiative. Canada had lost the kind of immunity from regional involvements that she had enjoyed in the early years of nationhood. Korea and Indo-China and Sinai were successive episodes that underlined the implications of Canada's position as an upholder of collective security and a foremost member in the ranks of the secondary states.

At the same time, such developments did not mean that the secondary states, once charged with these special responsibilities, were also vested with the power to decide or dispose of the issues that were involved. The Great Powers might not be all-powerful, but they had by no means abdicated. They still carried the decisive weight in world politics; they still provided the strength without whose backing their smaller associates would be largely ineffective. Canada might find herself drawn into new commitments, not only because her contribution was needed to supplement that of her larger associates, but as the result of a crisis created by their mistakes or misjudgments—factors over which she had little if any control. She had not only an important stake in the collective system as such—she had more than ever before a stake in the soundness of the individual policies pursued by her larger associates.

This meant, first and foremost, the policies of the United States. As a neighbor, the United States was of ever-increasing importance to Canada; as the leader of the Free World, its policies were now of almost daily concern to the mass of Canadian citizens.

Up to a point, the direct relations of the two countries followed much the same pattern as had developed during the past century or so. Friendship with the United States had throughout that period been a cardinal principle of Canadian policy. It had not always been easy to get the corresponding expressions of American good will translated into concrete measures, or to persuade Americans to treat Canada as an independent nation in her own right. The Good Neighbor policy of Franklin D. Roosevelt, however, ushered in a new phase in which Canada was accepted as an equal as well as a friend when it came to formal diplomatic dealings; and if on specific issues there were still grounds for complaints about lack of consideration for Canadian interests, these sprang rather from disparity in size than from any deliberate disregard of Canada's sovereign status.

What has occasionally been a matter for concern is the degree to which the actual exercise of sovereignty might be circumscribed by the growing influence of American interests over certain key aspects of Canada's national structure. This is both a consequence of the closer integration of the two countries during recent years and an illustration of the dominant place that the United States now occupies in the realm of external factors affecting Canadian policies and interests. The basic elements in the pattern may not have changed, but there have been striking changes in scale and shifts in emphasis; and in two spheres particularly—in economic relations and defense—there have been new developments that have significantly modified the shape of Canadian-American relations during the past decade.

Among the most consistent aspects of Canadian policy has been the constant effort to secure wider access to the American market. With the spectacular postwar upsurge of exports to the United States, it might seem paradoxical that the Canadian reaction was not so much satisfaction at this achievement as apprehension and irritation over American trade policies. There had been successive reductions in the American tariff since 1933, yet the persistence of protectionist pressures made for continual uncertainties about the future which were given substance by occasional concessions to American producers, either through increased duties or through quotas and embargoes. Moreover, while the American tariff structure in general favored the entry of Canadian primary products, it still raised barriers against manufactured goods, and Canadians who aimed at developing a national economy that would be more advanced as well as more diversified felt that the lines of evolution were being distorted by this imposition of stiff rates against their finished products. And although the fact that the United States took 60 per cent of Canada's exports might in one aspect be a cause for gratification, in another it increased Canadian uneasiness at this high degree of dependence on a more powerful neighbor over whose policies Canada had at best a very limited influence.

Added to the strains that arose in the direct relations of the two countries were the occasional points of friction resulting from their more general policies in the matter of world trade. In principle Canada and the United States were advocates of a lowering of trade barriers and a system of multilateral exchange. In practice it seemed at times that the United States was urging a strict adherence to these objectives by other countries while insisting on special exceptions for itself. The use of escape clauses not only had direct effects on Canadian exports such as minerals and dairy products; it also limited the contribution that the United States, as a creditor nation, needed to make to the world trade balance if a multilateral system was to be made freely operative. It meant that Canada's trade deficit with the United States, which in 1958 amounted to $1300 million, could not be fully offset by sales to other countries, since those countries in their turn found it hard to earn the dollars they needed by selling in a protected American market. And when the United States embarked on a policy of disposing of commodity surpluses by sales abroad on special terms, Canada felt that, besides being restricted in her ability to sell to the United States, she was being undercut by unfair practices in the alternative markets for her exports, especially the export of wheat. Taking it all in all, trade questions gave rise to the sharpest controversies between the two countries and provoked the stiffest protests from Canada against American policies.

Another major aspect of economic relations was the large-scale American investment in Canada during the postwar years. It was again paradoxical that this too gave rise to mixed feelings, though rather from apprehension over its political implications than from any serious resentment against American policies as such. There were occasional grounds for protest over such matters as the application of American laws to Canadian subsidiaries, but the real concern was over the extent to which key segments of the Canadian economy had fallen under outside control and the possibility that this might add a further element of distortion affecting the lines of Canadian economic development. This led every now and then to dark mutterings about the danger that economic infiltration might end by undermining Canadian sovereignty. It never resulted in concrete steps to restrict American investment, whose vital importance for the expansion of the Canadian economy was spectacularly evident, or even to use measures beyond persuasion and publicity to secure for Canadians a share in the direction of foreign-owned enterprises within their borders.

Similarly, in matters of defense, there were expressions of concern over the alleged attrition of Canada's independence accompanied in practice by a realistic acceptance of the demands of the actual situation. Of all the elements in postwar Canadian-American relations, this was the most novel as compared to the situation in the past. It was different not only in degree but in kind from the type of cooperation that even World War II had imposed. The nuclear-rocket age that staked the survival of the Free World on the striking power of the United States meant also that this power must be shielded from the long-range intercontinental blows to which it was now vulnerable. Canada's geographical position made her an essential element in the shield. The defense of North America was a continental problem that demanded integrated planning and operation. It was not enough for Canada to think in terms of protecting her own soil— she must collaborate to the maximum in the protection of the United States as the heartland of Western security. And if she could not fulfil this essential role on her own soil with her own resources, she must admit American supplementary activities within her own borders and the consequent American authority over such activities. As costs increased with advancing technology, so did the need to let the United States undertake the steps that Canada could not carry out by herself, and to provide the necessary facilities within Canada for the resulting American operations. The construction of the DEW Line, the creation of an integrated air defense through NORAD, the abandonment of the Arrow in favor of the BOMARC, were successive stages in the diminution of Canada's control of defense activities on and over her own soil; the acquisition of nuclear weapons or warheads will carry this a stage further. The problem of retaining effective sovereignty while agreeing to the concessions involved in this developing co-operation has not yet become acute, but it is evident that it lies implicit in this completely new relationship.

In another aspect, the progressive integration for purposes of defense illustrates the new level in relations that has developed during the past two decades. It is no longer merely a question of keeping Canada's separate policies in reasonable harmony with those of the United States and of minimizing any divergences that may arise in their respective courses of action in world affairs. The two countries are linked in common enterprises that call for joint rather than simply parallel action, and Canada has found herself obliged to consider positive efforts to act in concert with the United States to a far greater extent than ever in the past.

Involved in this development was a certain shift of emphasis from the United Kingdom to the United States as the main pole of Canada's external policy. This did not necessarily imply any diminution of Canada's attachment to Britain or any lessening of interest in Britain's position as a strong and stable factor in the world balance. It was simply an inevitable fact that the much greater power and resources of the United States had now been thrown actively into world affairs. Decisions that in the days of American isolation had to be taken without American participation now needed the consent and support of the United States if they were to be made effective. Support from Great Britain was still desirable and in some cases equally essential; but the power center of the Free World was now the United States, and neither Canada nor the other secondary nations could realistically ignore that salient fact.

Indeed, even the direct relations of Canada with her great neighbor, vital as they were to her national development, were at times overshadowed by concern over the policies pursued by the United States in the broader field of world affairs. This concern was not confined to questions with which Canada herself was associated, such as the efforts at disarmament or the development of NATO as an effective instrument of security. There were issues in which Canada was not directly involved and on which she differed sharply from the position of the United States, yet whose consequences she would inescapably share if they should take the form of a major conflict. The clearest example was the China policy of the United States, to which Canada specifically refused to pledge support, yet with full awareness that if American policy should lead to a full-scale war,

Canada could hardly stand aloof. The assumption by the United States of a leading role in world affairs gave Canada a powerful added incentive for maintaining the closest possible contact, and for using every available opportunity to influence American policy along lines that she could approve and support.

Perhaps those opportunities were not always used to the full. Perhaps, indeed, they were actually fewer than circumstances might at first lead one to expect. It could hardly be denied that if the United States was of paramount importance in Canadian eyes, Canada on her part was more than ever of real importance to the United States as a neighbor and customer and ally. Yet there were distinct limits to the use that could be made of this situation as a basis for pressure on Washington. There were few ways in which Canada could use her potential nuisance value without the risk that the harm might in the end be chiefly to herself. Threats by Canada of economic retaliation, of a refusal of defense facilities, of curtailing or withholding co-operation through NATO or the United Nations, were less likely to bring a change in American policies than to weaken the unity for common purposes that was one of the chief Canadian interests in the field of external affairs.

Here was a further illustration of how desirable it was for a Middle Power such as Canada to seek collective action wherever feasible as the most effective means for implementing her own policies in foreign affairs. The leverage that she could by herself exert on the policies of her larger associates was limited at best. She had to rely chiefly on reason and persuasion—qualities that were most likely to be effective when exercised in concert with others. By the same token, opportunities for the exercise of an effective initiative were more likely to present themselves under these conditions than they would to a smaller power acting in isolation. It may be that even in this wider sphere Canada was more diffident than she need have been about trying to give a lead. Partly this was a survival of the old habit of waiting for a lead from her larger associates; partly, too, it sprang from the realization that effective action could be taken only within the limits that those associates would accept, with a resulting tendency to wait until those limits were defined before trying to frame the kind of policy that would be practical and realistic. It is not impossible that a continued growth in maturity and national self-confidence may gradually overcome some of these inhibitions and stimulate a more forward policy on the part of Canada in the years ahead.

And here again it is the situation created by the cold war that provides the most likely incentive for such a development. The first problem was to find a way of preserving the free nations against the imminent threat, not only to their individual national existence, but to the survival of the kind of world within which they could continue to exist as the kind of nations they wanted to be. In this matter, Canada took a real initiative which made its contribution to the creation of NATO and the emergence of a collective system of Western defense. There is a continuing task of maintaining and strengthening that system, but along with that goes the need to search for means of relaxing the tensions that imperil world peace and stability, and ultimately of ending the cold war itself if that can be done by any means compatible with the preservation of the essential interests of the Free World. These are objectives that have been consistently inherent in Canada's foreign policy throughout the postwar years. She has lent support to all practical efforts toward these ends, whether through negotiations on disarmament or by efforts to strengthen the peace-preserving functions of the United Nations. As is her habit, she has tended to let the Great Powers play the foremost part in trying to work out a basis for agreement. Indeed, in matters in which she was not directly involved in the first instance, such as the question of a German settlement, she has been content mainly to put the expression of her interest on formal record, and has refrained from pressing for an active share in the immediate negotiations or from complicating matters by demanding a recognized status for herself. Nonetheless, she has made clear her desire for continued efforts at a rapprochement with the Soviet bloc and for a serious exploration of every advance, however unpromising, that comes from that quarter. In this she has been against the attitude of rigidity and rejection that some of her associates have at times exhibited, and has been prepared to recognize that mutual concessions may be the necessary price for a genuine appeasement in the true sense of that much-abused word. It is very possible that the Berlin crisis marked the opening of a new phase in which consolidation and adjustment will be the dominant themes in international relations, and in which the imagination as well as the tenacity of national leaders will have to be exercised to the utmost. There is no likelihood that this will bring any change in the basic aims that Canada has traditionally pursued, or in the identity of her fundamental objectives with those of her traditional associates, or in the closeness of co-operation with her historic partners in world affairs. The real task will once again be to work out the most favorable adaptation to changing conditions; and Canada, whose postwar policies have by no means been devoid of flexibility, may yet find new and still wider scope for a constructive application of that quality in the phase that lies before us.

Selected Readings on Canadian External Policy, 1909-1959

Gaddis Smith

The very idea that there exists such a phenomenon as Canadian external policy has enjoyed wide acceptance for little more than a generation. It is not surprising, therefore, that the literature on the subject, although voluminous, is still full of gaps and is all too often of rapidly passing interest. A systematic and detailed study of the last half century of Canadian external policy broadly based on unpublished as well as public printed sources is yet to be written. Furthermore, comparatively few of the many significant episodes of a half century have been subjected in scholarly articles to the searching examination they deserve. However, as more rich collections of the private papers of Canadian twentieth-century statesmen become available for study in the Public Archives of Canada, Ottawa, and in other repositories, the existing lacuna will quickly be filled. Someday also the files of the Department of External Affairs, now completely closed, will begin to open. For the historical study of Canadian external policy the dawn is just commencing to break.

In no country is it possible to draw a line and say, "Here is the boundary of external policy; all else belongs to domestic affairs." This impossibility is especially marked in Canada, a country where every aspect of national life including agriculture, industry, social attitudes, politics, and constitutional development are conditioned to an unusual degree by external factors. Virtually every work on Canada, therefore, has some relevance to external affairs. But the list which follows is extremely, almost ruthlessly, selective. It is intended as the merest introduction to a few major titles. No attempt has been made to deal with the thousands of periodical articles that make up the bulk of the writing on external affairs.

1. Guides

Although there is no single bibliographical guide to the study of Canadian external affairs, the pages of the *Canadian Historical Review*, the *Canadian Journal of Economics and Political Science*, and the *International Journal* together note the publication of and often comment on books and articles relating to external affairs. These periodicals—founded respectively in 1920, 1935, and 1946—have themselves published the majority of the noteworthy articles on external affairs appearing since World War I. Each issue of the *Canadian Historical Review* contains an extensive listing of "Recent Publications Relating to Canada" including sections on Commonwealth and international affairs. Each year the *Canadian Historical Review* also publishes a review article on "Canada and Commonwealth Affairs." A companion review article on "Canada and Foreign Affairs" appeared annually from 1935 to 1951. The *Review* in addition prints an annual list of doctoral and master's theses on Canadian history and related subjects in preparation at Canadian, American, and Commonwealth universities. A useful survey of the literature appearing before 1949 is G. P. deT. Glazebrook, "Canadian Foreign Policy in the Twentieth Century," *Journal of Modern History*, XXI (March, 1949), 44-55. K. W. McNaught, "Canadian Foreign Policy and the Whig Interpretation," *Annual Report of the Canadian Historical Association*, *1957*, 43-54, is a provocative essay describing a bias which the author feels has long inhibited the writing of Canadian history. *External Affairs*, the official monthly bulletin of the Department of External Affairs, provides a guide to government publications.

2. General

The only general survey of external affairs from the years of New France to the Cold War is G. P. deT. Glazebrook, *A History of Canadian External Relations* (Toronto, 1950). Although much in need of revision, this book is indispensable. The Glazebrook *History* was issued under the auspices of the Canadian Institute of International Affairs, as have been an extraordinarily large proportion of the book-length studies of the different aspects of Canadian external affairs. This vigorous institution, established in 1928, is the single most important agency for extending knowledge of Canada's external affairs. In addition to its book publishing program, the Institute sponsors the quarterly, *International Journal*, issues timely pamphlets, provides a library service, and covers Canada with a network of local chapters. One of the early books published under the Institute's auspices was Robert Alexander MacKay and E. B. Rogers,

Canada Looks Abroad (Toronto, 1938). This volume attempted with considerable success to describe the social, political, and economic roots of Canadian external policy as they existed in the 1930's. After two cataclysmic decades another ambitious undertaking of this nature is needed. *Canada Looks Abroad* was the foundation stone on which has been placed a continuing series of volumes each surveying a two or three year interval of *Canada in World Affairs* (Toronto, 1941—). The survey volumes published to date are: F. H. Soward, and others, *The Pre-War Years* (1941); R. MacGregor Dawson, *Two Years of War, 1939-1941* (1943); C. Cecil Lingard and Reginald G. Trotter, *September 1941 to May 1944* (1950); F. H. Soward, *From Normandy to Paris, 1944-1946* (1950); Robert A. Spencer, *From UN to NATO, 1946-1949* (1959); W. E. C. Harrison, *1949-1950* (1957); B. S. Keirstead, *September 1951 to October 1953* (1956); Donald C. Masters, *1953 to 1955* (1959); and James George Eayrs, *October 1955 to June 1957* (1959).

John Bartlet Brebner, *North Atlantic Triangle: the Interplay of Canada, the United States and Great Britain* (New Haven, 1945) is a classic and seminal work which must be included in any discussion of the literature of Canadian external relations. A. Gordon Dewey, *The Dominions and Diplomacy: The Canadian Contribution* (2 vols.; Toronto, 1929) is an over-long examination primarily of Canada's relations with Great Britain from 1887 to 1926. It is still useful because of copious quotations from newspapers and public government documents, the sources from which it is written. Mason Wade, *The French Canadians* (Toronto, 1955) is a massive look at its subject. Long chapters on the twentieth century contain much material on the French Canadian external outlook. H. Gordon Skilling, *Canadian Representation Abroad* (Toronto, 1945) is a useful survey. A supplement dealing with the growth of Canadian overseas representation since 1945 is much needed, as is a full study of the Department of External Affairs.

3. The Commonwealth

The flow of writings on the Commonwealth and Canada's relation thereto has long been at flood stage. Frank H. Underhill, *The British Commonwealth* (Durham, N. C., 1956) is a graceful introduction to which is appended a fine short bibliography. Indispensable are William Keith Hancock, *Survey of British Commonwealth Affairs*, Vol. I, *Problems of Nationality, 1918-1936;* Vol. II, *Problems of Economic Policy, 1918-1939* (London, 1937 and 1942), and the two magnificent studies by Nicholas Mansergh, *Survey of British Commonwealth Affairs: Problems of External Policy, 1918-1939* (London, 1952) and *Problems of*

Wartime Co-operation and Post War Change, 1939-1952 (London, 1958). Robert MacGregor Dawson, *The Development of Dominion Status, 1900-1936* (Toronto, 1937) is a well-known and convenient commentary and documentary collection on the course of Canada's constitutional progress within the Empire-Commonwealth. Heather J. Harvey, *Consultation and Co-operation in the Commonwealth* (London, 1952) is a handbook on the procedure of Commonwealth relations. An earlier volume under the same title was published in 1934. Gwendolen Margaret Carter, *The British Commonwealth and International Security: The Role of the Dominions, 1919-1939* (Toronto, 1947) is an analysis of the reaction of the Commonwealth, with particular emphasis on Canada, to the "twenty years truce." The tale it tells so well is not a stirring one.

4. The United States

The volume of writings on the Commonwealth is rivaled only by the outpouring, much of it ephemeral, on the relations between Canada and the United States. The two soundest single volume treatments of the subject are Edgar W. McInnis, *The Unguarded Frontier: A History of American-Canadian Relations* (Toronto, 1942) and Hugh L. Keenleyside and Gerald S. Brown, *Canada and the United States: Aspects of their Historical Relations* (New York, 1952), a revision of Keenleyside's 1929 volume. An eternal monument to Canadian-American scholarly cooperation is the twenty-five volume series on "The Relations of Canada and the United States" published between 1936 and 1945 under the sponsorship of the Carnegie Endowment for International Peace. James T. Shotwell was the general editor. The volumes treat of the social, economic, and political relations of the two countries and are generally of high quality. John S. Galbraith, *The Establishment of Canadian Diplomatic Status at Washington* (Berkeley, 1951) is a competent monograph. R. Warren James, *Wartime Economic Co-operation* (Toronto, 1949) deals with the relations of the two countries during World War II. Much journalistic ink, often alarmist in color, has been spilled on the subject of tension between the United States and Canada. Two interesting examples, reflecting the climate of opinion at the time of publication, are John MacCormac, *Canada: America's Problem* (New York, 1940) and James Barber, *Good Fences Make Good Neighbors: Why the United States Provokes Canadians* (Toronto, 1958).

5. From World War I to Cold War

There is no single treatment of Canada and World War I. This is one of the greatest gaps in the literature of Canadian external affairs.

Two books deal with the major problems facing Canada externally on the eve of war: commercial relations with the United States and naval co-operation with Great Britain. They are L. Ethan Ellis, *Reciprocity, 1911* (New Haven, 1939) and Gilbert N. Tucker, *The Naval Service of Canada*, Vol. I, *Origins and Early Years* (Ottawa, 1952). Two biography-memoirs deal imperfectly with the wartime Prime Minister and the leader of the opposition: Henry Borden, ed., *Robert Laird Borden: His Memoirs* (2 vols.; Toronto, 1938) and Oscar Douglas Skelton, *The Life and Letters of Sir Wilfrid Laurier* (2 vols.; Toronto, 1921). G. P. deT. Glazebrook has written a succinct monograph on *Canada at the Paris Peace Conference* (Toronto, 1942). R. MacGregor Dawson, *William Lyon Mackenzie King: A Political Biography*, Vol. I, *1874-1923* (Toronto, 1958) is a handsome and detailed beginning to Mackenzie King's official biography, not equal in sprightliness to Bruce Hutchinson's popular *The Incredible Canadian: A Candid Portrait of Mackenzie King* (Toronto, 1952).

S. Mack Eastman, *Canada at Geneva: A Historical Survey and Its Lessons* (Toronto, 1946) is the best study of Canada and the League of Nations. Also see the personal memoir of Walter Alexander Riddell, *World Security by Conference* (Toronto, 1947). Jean Pierre Després has written an account of *Le Canada et l'Organisation Internationale du Travail* (Montreal, 1947). F. H. Soward and A. M. Macauley have dealt briefly with *Canada and the Pan American System* (Toronto, 1948).

Three volumes deal with Canada and the Far East. Charles J. Woodsworth, *Canada and the Orient* (Toronto, 1941) treats its subject in broad perspective but needs to be brought up to date. A. R. M. Lower, *Canada and the Far East—1940* (New York, 1940) is hastily written and reflects the mounting tension which preceded the outbreak of World War II in the Pacific. H. F. Angus continues the account of *Canada and the Far East, 1940-1953* (Toronto, 1953). Raymond Arthur Davies, *Canada and Russia: Neighbors and Friends* (Toronto, 1944) is slim, journalistic, and mirrors the optimism of the wartime period. A scholarly study of Canada's relations with Russia is sorely needed.

F. H. Soward and Edgar McInnis have together summarized the activities of *Canada and the United Nations* (New York, 1957) while Edgar McInnis alone has recently published a sage essay on *The Atlantic Triangle and the Cold War* (Toronto, 1959).

INDEX

l'Action Catholique, 119
l'Action nationale, 116
Aeronautics Case, 89, 92
Aid, foreign. *See* foreign aid
Aitken, Max. *See* Lord Beaverbrook
Alderson, General Edwin, 45, 46
American-Canadian relations, 103, 104, 108, 112, 124, 125, 129
Anderson, John, 15
Anglo-American understanding, importance of to Canada, 104
Anti-Americanism, 107, 124-130 *passim*
Anti-conscriptionism. *See* Military conscription
Appeasement, policy of toward Germany, 72-75
Article X (League of Nations Covenant), French-Canadian attitude toward, 111
Asquith, Herbert, 41
Atkin, Lord (James R.), 86, 86 n., 89, 93
Atlantic Community, 126
Atomic Energy Control Act (1946), 93
Attorney General for Ontario v. Scott, 90-91
Auden, W. H., 60 n.
Aylesworth, Allen, 22 n., 29

Balfour Agreement, 8, 105 n.
Balfour Report, 153, 155
Beaudry, Laurent, 67, 105 n.
Beaverbrook, Lord (Aitken, Max), 46, 59 n.
Bennett, Prime Minister Richard B., 10, 45 n., 59, 112
Blacklock, T. H., 40 n.
Blanchette, J. H., 115
Bloc populaire Canadien, 118
BOMARC, 159
Borden, Prime Minister Robert, 8, 35, 36, 46, 47, 48, 48 n., 111 n., 136;

and changes in act to create Dept. of External Affairs (*q.v.*), 25-27 *passim*; and relations with Britain over industry during World War I, 39-44 *passim*; and policy toward U. S., 50-53 *passim*, 58; and Siberian intervention, 54-56 *passim*; and Canadian sovereignty as object of external policy, 57-58
Bourassa, Henri, 102, 111, 112
Brebner, John Bartlet, 109, 124
Bretton Woods Conference, 106 n.
British imperialism, 102, 109, 110, 114
British North America Act (1867), 90, 91, 92; and provision for treaty power (Section 132), 82-84, 85-88 *passim*; and rights of provinces (Section 92), 87, 88. *See also* Treaty power
Brodeur, L. P., 17
Bruchési, Jean, 113
Bryce, James, 15 n., 26, 30, 31; and support for creation of Dept. of Foreign Affairs, 21-23

Cahan, C. H., 10
Calhoun, John C., 104, 123 n.
Canadian-American Boundary Waters Treaty (1909), 94, 95
Canadian-American Reciprocity Treaty (1854), 83
Canadian Annual Review, 64
Canadian Bill of Rights, proposed, 92
Canadian Pacific Ocean Services, 44
Canadian War Mission, 52
Canadian War Records Office, 46
Canadianism: defined, 123; contrasted with Americanism, 124; possibilities for, 128
Cardin, Lucien, 129
Carnegie, Colonel David, 42 n.
Cartier, George Etienne, 104

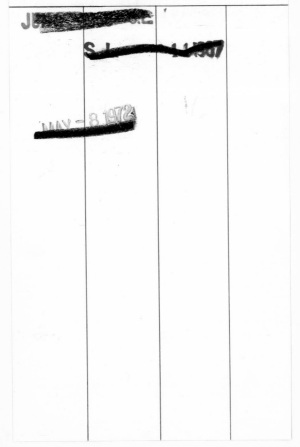